USWORTH COLLEGE

U05927

√7/05

A GUIDE TO

MACBETH

STEVE EDDY

WITH TONY BUZAN

Ref
ELI
822.33
EDD

CITY OF
SUNDERLAND
COLLEGE

LEARNING CENTRE
SHINEY ROW

FOR
REFERENCE ONLY

Hodder & Stoughton

D1151364

Cover photograph ©: The Ronald Grant Archive
Mind Maps: David Orr
Illustrations: Karen Donnelly; Julian Mosedale

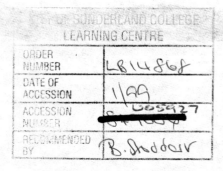

SUNDERLAND COLLEGE LEARNING CENTRE	
ORDER NUMBER	LB14868
DATE OF ACCESSION	1/99
ACCESSION NUMBER	665927
RECOMMENDED BY	B. Stoddair

Orders: please contact Bookpoint Ltd, 39 Milton Park, Abingdon, Oxon OX14 4TD.
Telephone: (44) 01235 400414, Fax: (44) 01235 400454. Lines are open from 9.00 –
6.00, Monday to Saturday, with a 24 hour message answering service. Email address:
orders@bookpoint.co.uk

British Library Cataloguing in Publication Data
A catalogue record for this title is available from The British Library

ISBN 0 340 66397 9

First published 1998
Impression number   11 10 9 8 7 6 5 4 3 2
Year   2004 2003 2002 2001 2000 1999 1998

The 'Teach Yourself' name and logo are registered trade marks of
Hodder & Stoughton Ltd.

Copyright © 1998 Steve Eddy
Introduction ('How to study') copyright © 1998 Tony Buzan

All rights reserved. No part of this publication may be reproduced or transmitted in
any form or by any means, electronic or mechanical, including photocopy, recording,
or any information storage and retrieval system, without permission in writing from
the publisher or under licence from the Copyright Licensing Agency Limited.
Further details of such licences (for reprographic reproduction) may be obtained
from the Copyright Licensing Agency Limited, of 90 Tottenham Court Road,
London W1P 9HE.

Typeset by Transet Limited, Coventry, England.
Printed in Great Britain for Hodder & Stoughton Educational, a division of
Hodder Headline Plc, 338 Euston Road, London NW1 3BH by Cox and Wyman Ltd,
Reading, Berks.

CONTENTS

How to study   **v**

How to use this guide   **ix**

Key to icons   **x**

Background   **1**
- A play for James I   1
- The Divine Right of Kings   1
- Witchcraft   1

The story of *Macbeth*   **2**

Who's who?   **8**
- Macbeth: evil 'hero' who becomes
  King of Scotland   8
- Lady Macbeth: his wife – the power
  behind the throne   13
- Banquo: an honourable general and
  father of kings   15
- Macduff: a brave nobleman loyal to Duncan   16
- Duncan: the old King, murdered by Macbeth   18
- Malcolm: Duncan's son and heir   18
- Minor characters: Lady Macduff, Ross,
  Lennox, Fleance   18

Themes and imagery   **21**
- Disorder   21
- Sickness and health   22
- The supernatural   23
- Light and dark   24
- Appearances   25
- Courage   26
- Sleep   27
- Time   28

Commentary   **31**
- ●Act 1   31
- ●Act 2   40
- ●Act 3   46
- ●Act 4   54
- ●Act 5   62

Topics for discussion and brainstorming   **74**

How to get an 'A' in English Literature   **75**

The exam essay   **76**

Model answer and essay plans   **77**

Glossary of literary terms   **83**

Index   **85**

HOW TO STUDY

There are five important things you must know about your brain and memory to revolutionise the way you study:

◆ how your memory ('recall') works *while* you are learning
◆ how your memory works *after* you have finished learning
◆ how to use Mind Maps – a special technique for helping you with all aspects of your studies
◆ how to increase your reading speed
◆ how to prepare for tests and exams.

Recall during learning
– THE NEED FOR BREAKS

When you are studying, your memory can concentrate, understand and remember well for between 20 and 45 minutes at a time. Then it needs a break. If you carry on for longer than this without a break your memory starts to break down. If you study for hours non-stop, you will remember only a small fraction of what you have been trying to learn, and you will have wasted hours of valuable time.

So, ideally, *study for less than an hour*, then take a five to ten minute break. During the break listen to music, go for a walk, do some exercise, or just daydream. (Daydreaming is a necessary brain-power booster – geniuses do it regularly.) During the break your brain will be sorting out what it has been learning, and you will go back to your books with the new information safely stored and organised in your memory banks. We recommend breaks at regular intervals as you work through the Literature Guides. Make sure you take them!

Recall after learning
– THE WAVES OF YOUR MEMORY

What do you think begins to happen to your
memory straight after you have finished learning something?
Does it immediately start forgetting? No! Your brain actually
increases its power and carries on remembering. For a short
time after your study session, your brain integrates the
information, making a more complete picture of everything it
has just learnt. Only then does the rapid decline in memory
begin, and as much as 80 per cent of what you have learnt can
be forgotten in a day.

However, if you catch the top of the wave of your memory,
and briefly review (look back over) what you have been
studying at the correct time, the memory is stamped in far more
strongly, and stays at the crest of the wave for a much longer
time. To maximise your brain's power to remember, take a few
minutes and use a Mind Map to review what you have learnt
at the end of a day. Then review it at the end of a week, again
at the end of a month, and finally a week before your test or
exam. That way you'll ride your memory
wave all the way there – and beyond!

The Mind Map ®
– A PICTURE OF THE WAY YOU THINK

Do you like taking notes? More importantly, do you like having to
go back over and learn them before tests or exams? Most
students I know certainly do not! And how do you take your
notes? Most people take notes on lined paper, using blue or
black ink. The result, visually, is boring! And what does *your* brain
do when it is bored? It turns off, tunes out, and goes to sleep!
Add a dash of colour, rhythm, imagination, and the whole note-
taking process becomes much more fun, uses more of your
brain's abilities, and improves your recall and understanding.

A Mind Map mirrors the way your brain works. It can be used
for note-taking from books or in class, for reviewing what you
have just studied, and for essay planning for coursework and
in tests or exams. It uses all your memory's natural techniques
to build up your rapidly growing 'memory muscle'.

You will find Mind Maps throughout this book. Study them, add some colour, personalise them, and then have a go at drawing your own – you'll remember them far better! Stick them in your files and on your walls for a quick-and-easy review of the topic.

HOW TO DRAW A MIND MAP

1 Start in the middle of the page. This gives your brain the maximum room for its thoughts.
2 Always start by drawing a small picture or symbol. Why? Because a picture is worth a thousand words to your brain. And try to use at least three colours, as colour helps your memory even more.
3 Let your thoughts flow, and write or draw your ideas on coloured branching lines connected to your central image. These key symbols and words are the headings for your topic. Start like the Mind Map on page 8.
4 Then add facts and ideas by drawing more, smaller, branches on to the appropriate main branches, just like a tree.
5 Always print your word clearly on its line. Use only one word per line.
6 To link ideas and thoughts on different branches, use arrows, colours, underlining, and boxes (see page 12).

HOW TO READ A MIND MAP

1 Begin in the centre, the focus of your topic.
2 The words/images attached to the centre are like chapter headings, read them next.
3 Always read out from the centre, in every direction (even on the left-hand side, where you will have to read from right to left, instead of the usual left to right).

USING MIND MAPS

Mind Maps are a versatile tool – use them for taking notes in class or from books, for solving problems, for brainstorming with friends, and for reviewing and working for tests or exams – their uses are endless! You will find them invaluable for planning essays for coursework and exams. Number your main branches in the order in which you want to use them and off you go – the main headings for your essay are done and all your ideas are logically organised!

Super speed reading

It seems incredible, but it's been proved – the faster you read, the more you understand and remember! So here are some tips to help you to practise reading faster – you'll cover the ground more quickly, remember more, and have more time left for both work and play.

♦ First read the whole text (whether it's a lengthy book or an exam or test paper) very quickly, to give your brain an overall idea of what's ahead and get it working. (It's like sending out a scout to look at the territory you have to cover – it's much easier when you know what to expect!) Then read the text again for more detailed information.
♦ Have the text a reasonable distance away from your eyes. In this way your eye/brain system will be able to see more at a glance, and will naturally begin to read faster.
♦ Take in groups of words at a time. Rather than reading 'slowly and carefully' read faster, more enthusiastically.
♦ Take in phrases rather than single words while you read.
♦ Use a guide. Your eyes are designed to follow movement, so a thin pencil underneath the lines you are reading, moved smoothly along, will 'pull' your eyes to faster speeds.

Preparing for tests and exams

♦ Review your work systematically. Cram at the start of your course, not the end, and avoid 'exam panic'!
♦ Use Mind Maps throughout your course, and build a Master Mind Map for each subject – a giant Mind Map that summarises everything you know about the subject.
♦ Use memory techniques such as mnemonics (verses or systems for remembering things like dates and events).
♦ Get together with one or two friends to study, compare Mind Maps, and discuss topics.

AND FINALLY...

Have *fun* while you learn – it has been shown that students who make their studies enjoyable understand and remember everything better and get the highest grades. I wish you and your brain every success! ──(Tony Buzan)

HOW TO USE THIS GUIDE

The guide assumes that you have already read *Macbeth*, although you could read 'Background' and 'The story of *Macbeth*' before reading the play. It is best to use the guide alongside the text. You could read the 'Who's who?' and 'Themes and imagery' sections without referring to the text, but you will get more out of these sections if you do refer to the text to check points made in these sections for yourself, and especially when thinking about the questions designed to test your recall and help you to think about the play.

The 'Commentary' section can be used in a number of ways. One way is to read a scene in the play, and then read the commentary for that scene. Keep on until you come to a test box, test yourself – then have a break! Alternatively, read the commentary for a scene, or several scenes, then read the scenes in the play, then go back to the commentary.

'Topics for discussion and brainstorming' gives topics that could well feature in exams or provide the basis for coursework. It would be particularly useful for you to discuss them with friends, or brainstorm them using Mind Map techniques (see p. vi).

'How to get an "A" in English Literature' gives valuable advice on what to look for in any text, and what skills you need to develop in order to achieve your personal best.

'The exam essay' is a useful reminder of how to tackle exam questions, and 'Model answer and essay plans' gives examples of an 'A'-grade essay and other essay plans – which you could expand into essays.

The questions

Whenever you come across a question in the guide with a star ✪ in front of it, think about it for a moment. You could even jot down a few words in rough to focus your mind. There is not usually a 'right' answer to these questions: it is important for you to develop your own opinions if you want to get an 'A' in your exam. The test sections are designed to take you about 10–20 minutes each – which will be time well spent.

EY TO ICONS

Themes and imagery

A **theme** is an idea explored by an author. **Imagery** refers to the kind of word picture used to make the idea come alive. Particular sorts of image are usually associated with each theme. Whenever a theme is dealt with in the guide, the appropriate icon is used. This means you can find where a theme is mentioned just by flicking through the book. Go on – try it now!

Disorder   Appearances

Sickness and health   Courage

The supernatural   Sleep

Light and dark   Time

 STYLE AND LANGUAGE

This heading and icon are used in the Commentary wherever there is a special section on the author's choice of words and use of literary devices.

ACKGROUND

A *play for James I*

We often call the people of Shakespeare's time 'the Elizabethans', but in fact *Macbeth* was written after the death of Queen Elizabeth I. On her deathbed, unmarried and childless, she had named as her successor James VI of Scotland. He became James I of England.

Shakespeare wrote the play with the new king in mind. He took the basic story from *The Chronicles of Scotland*, a history book by Raphael Holinshed, but he changed a lot of the details. The real-life Banquo was guilty, but since he was an ancestor of James I, Shakespeare makes him innocent in the play.

The *Divine Right of kings*

James I believed in the Divine Right of kings – that kings were appointed by God. This was accepted by most people, probably including Shakespeare. Therefore, killing a king would be far worse than an ordinary murder. James wrote at length about the role of kings, including their responsibilities.

James believed that God had allowed him to inherit the healing powers of Edward the Confessor – the Edward in the play. The passage in the play about these powers (Act 4, scene 3) is not really necessary to the plot, and was probably to flatter James.

Witchcraft

Shakespeare's audience believed in God and the devil, and in heaven and hell as real places. They also believed in evil spirits, in possession by spirits, and in the power of witchcraft and magic. James I himself was especially interested in the subject, and wrote a book about it, *Daemonologie*.

Women suspected of witchcraft were often illegally tortured. If found guilty they were hanged, in England, or burnt at the stake, in other countries. One Scottish woman, Agnes Sampson, was accused of trying to kill James by witchcraft. She was supposed to have attached parts of a dead body to a cat, sailed to sea in a sieve, and put the cat in the sea to cause a storm to wreck the King's ship.

connections between events

1 Witches plan to meet Macbeth

2 Duncan hears how Macbeth and Banquo have led his army to victory

3 Witches predict Macbeth will be Thane of Cawdor, and Banquo will father a line of kings

4 Duncan makes Macbeth Thane of Cawdor and makes Malcolm heir to throne

5 Lady Macbeth persuades Macbeth to kill Duncan and he does

6 Murder discovered. Malcolm and Donalbain decide to flee

7 Macbeth has Banquo killed

8 Banquo's ghost appears at banquet

9 Witches show Macbeth apparitions

10 Macbeth has Macduff's family killed

11 Malcom tests Macduff's loyalty at English court

12 Malcom leads army to Scotland. Macbeth prepares army for battle

13 Lady Macbeth's madness and suicide

14 Macduff kills Macbeth in battle. Macduff becomes King

THE STORY OF *MACBETH*

Act 1 *Prediction*

Three **Witches** plan to meet **Macbeth** on a desolate heath. King **Duncan** is **delighted** to hear of the victory bravely achieved by **Macbeth** and **Banquo** against the treacherous Thane of Cawdor and Macdonwald, and the Norwegians.

Macbeth and Banquo meet the **Witches**, who **predict** that Macbeth will be Thane of **Cawdor**, then **King**, while Banquo's **descendants** will be kings. Macbeth is amazed, Banquo disbelieving. **Duncan** makes Macbeth Thane of Cawdor, has the old Thane of Cawdor executed, and names Malcolm **successor** to the throne.

Lady Macbeth reads Macbeth's **letter** about the Witches, hears that **Duncan** is **coming**, and immediately starts to **plan** his murder. Macbeth returns home, and Duncan **arrives**. Macbeth decides not to murder Duncan, but Lady Macbeth taunts him and changes his mind again.

Act 2 *Murder*

Banquo and **Fleance** meet **Macbeth** at night. Macbeth thinks fearfully about the coming **murder**, sees a vision of a dagger, and goes to do the awful deed. Afterwards he's terrified by his crime. Lady Macbeth tries to calm him down, and returns the bloody daggers to Duncan's chamber.

By now it's morning, and **Macduff** and **Lennox** are hammering at the castle gate. The **Porter** lets them in and jokes with them. Duncan's murder is **discovered**. Macbeth kills Duncan's **servants**. Malcolm and Donalbain decide to flee.

Ross and an Old Man discuss the strange and unnatural events of the night before. Macduff brings news that Duncan's sons have fled, and that **Macbeth** has been **chosen** as **king**.

Act 3 *Banquet*

Banquo thinks about the Witches' predictions and accepts Macbeth's invitation to a **banquet**. Macbeth tells himself that he has to kill Banquo and Fleance. He engages murderers to kill them, but only hints at this to Lady Macbeth. **Banquo** is **stabbed** to death, Fleance **escapes**.

At the banquet, Macbeth is terrified by Banquo's **ghost**. In the end Lady Macbeth asks the guests to leave.

Hecate, goddess of the night, meets the Witches.

We hear that Malcolm is in the court of the virtuous King **Edward** of England, and that Macduff has gone there to ask for help in **overthrowing** Macbeth.

Act 4 *Division*

The Witches show Macbeth apparitions that convince him that he cannot be harmed, but that Banquo's descendants will still be kings. Macbeth decides to kill Macduff's wife and children.

In a touching scene, **Lady Macduff** discusses her husband with her **son**. Then mother and son are cruelly **murdered**.

Malcolm tests Macduff's loyalty, then describes King Edward's healing powers. Macduff almost breaks down when he hears about his family's massacre.

Act 5 *End*

Lady Macbeth seems to have been driven mad by her guilt. She walks and talks in her sleep. A doctor says he can't cure her.

The grimly determined Macbeth and his enemies prepare for battle. Malcolm orders his soldiers to disguise themselves with tree branches.

The tormented **Lady Macbeth** commits **suicide**. A messenger tells Macbeth that **Birnam wood** is approaching – Malcolm's army.

The battle begins. In a final showdown, Macduff **kills Macbeth** in the battle, and Malcolm is hailed as the new king.

HOW WELL HAVE YOU REMEMBERED THE PLOT?

See if you can fill in the keywords in the blanks on the next
two pages without looking back. Then check how you've done.

Act 1 *Prediction*

Three _____ plan to meet _____ on a desolate heath. King
_____ is _____ to hear of the _____ bravely achieved by
_____ and _____ against the treacherous Thane of Cawdor
and Macdonwald, and the Norwegians.

   Macbeth and Banquo meet the _____, who _____ that
Macbeth will be Thane of _____, then _____, while
Banquo's _____ will be kings. Macbeth is amazed, Banquo
disbelieving. _____ makes Macbeth Thane of Cawdor, has the
old Thane of Cawdor executed, and names Malcolm _____ to
the throne.

   Lady Macbeth reads Macbeth's _____ about the Witches,
hears that _____ is _____, and immediately starts to
_____ his murder. Macbeth returns home, and
Duncan _____. Macbeth decides not to murder Duncan, but
Lady Macbeth taunts him and changes his mind again.

Act 2 *Murder*

_____ and _____ meet _____ at night. Macbeth thinks
fearfully about the coming _____, sees a vision of a _____,
and goes to do the awful deed. Afterwards he's terrified by his
crime. Lady Macbeth tries to calm him down, and returns the
bloody daggers to Duncan's chamber.

   By now it's morning, and _____ and _____ are
hammering at the castle gate. The _____ lets them in and
jokes with them. Duncan's murder is _____. Macbeth kills
Duncan's _____. Malcolm and Donalbain decide to flee.

   Ross and an Old Man discuss the strange and unnatural
events of the night before. Macduff brings news that Duncan's
sons have fled, and that _____ has been _____ as _____.

Act 3 *Banquet*

Banquo thinks about the Witches' predictions and accepts Macbeth's invitation to a _____. Macbeth tells himself that he has to kill Banquo and Fleance. He engages murderers to kill them, but only hints at this to Lady Macbeth. _____ is_____ to death, Fleance_____.

At the banquet, Macbeth is terrified by Banquo's _____. In the end Lady Macbeth asks the guests to leave.

Hecate, goddess of the night, meets the Witches.

We hear that Malcolm is in the court of the virtuous King _____ of England, and that Macduff has gone there to ask for help in _____ Macbeth.

Act 4 *Division*

The Witches show Macbeth _____ that convince him that he cannot be harmed, but that Banquo's descendants will still be kings. Macbeth decides to kill Macduff's wife and children.

In a touching scene, _____ _____ discusses her husband with her _____. Then mother and son are cruelly _____.

Malcolm tests Macduff's loyalty, then describes King Edward's healing powers. Macduff almost breaks down when he hears about his family's massacre.

Act 5 *End*

_____ _____ seems to have been driven _____ by her guilt. She walks and talks in her sleep. A doctor says he can't cure her.

The grimly determined Macbeth and his enemies prepare for battle. Malcolm orders his soldiers to disguise themselves with _____ _____.

The tormented _____ _____ commits _____. A messenger tells Macbeth that _____ _____ is approaching – Malcolm's army.

The battle begins. In a final showdown, Macduff_____ _____ in the battle, and Malcolm is hailed as the new king.

WHO'S WHO?

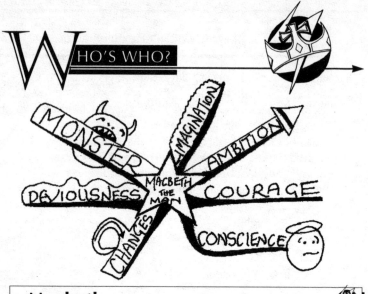

Macbeth

Before you read about Macbeth, look at the Mini Mind Map above for a preview of his character. As you read on, think about the following questions. Try to form your own opinions.

♦ What are his strengths and weaknesses?
♦ Is he an evil man, or a victim of evil?
♦ Does he have an unhealthy need to prove his manhood?
♦ Is he weaker than his wife?
♦ Why does he murder Duncan despite not wanting to?
♦ How does he change?
♦ How might he be seen as a **tragic hero** (someone we admire and sympathise with, and whose downfall and death are caused by a weakness in their character combined with fate)?

Courage

The first impression we have of Macbeth is from the Sergeant (or 'Captain') in Act 1, scene 2. He is *brave Macbeth*, who has ripped Macdonwald open from navel to jaw. He is a man of fierce and bloody action. Do you see him as a hero or a butcher?

Macbeth can be brave only when he knows what to do and feels justified in doing it. He feels like this at the beginning and end of the play, but in between he is prey to doubts and fears.

We first see him afraid when the thought of murdering Duncan initially occurs to him (Act 1, scene 3, lines 134–42). It makes his hair stand on end and his heart pound. In Act 2, scene 1, in his *Is this a dagger ...* speech (lines 33–64), he is horrified at the murder he is to commit, afraid that even the stones he walks on will give him away.

In *Act 2, scene 2*, after the murder, he is almost hysterical. In his fear he has brought the daggers away from Duncan's chamber and cannot bring himself to return them. Lady Macbeth has to do it for him. In the banquet scene (Act 3, scene 4), he's terrified of Banquo's ghost.

Only at the end of the play is he again the fearless man of action: *I have almost forgot the taste of fears* (Act 5, scene 5). In his final speech, all but beaten, he cries, *Yet I will try my last.* ✪ Do you admire his determination to go down fighting?

A *real man*

Macbeth is very concerned with being a real man. ✪ What do you consider to be the qualities of 'a real man'?

Frightened by his first murderous thoughts, he says that the fear shakes his *single state of man*. Lady Macbeth, knowing her husband well, gets him to murder Duncan by calling him a coward. At first he defends himself: *I dare do all that may become a man;/ Who dares do more, is none.* He means that the crime would be inhuman. But in the end she convinces him (Act 1, scene 7).

✪ Macbeth is terrified by Banquo's ghost, but is he even more disturbed by his own fear, because it makes him doubt his manhood? He says, *What man dare, I dare,* and insists that if the ghost takes the shape of a wild animal, he will face it without trembling. When it goes, he says, *I am a man again.* He can face physical threat, but not guilt or the supernatural.

Conscience

Macbeth knows that killing a king is a terrible crime. At the start of Act 1, scene 7, he considers whether to do it. When he thinks of the moral objections (*see* 'Commentary' p. 38), he decides to *proceed no further in this business* – until Lady Macbeth changes his mind again.

He is reluctant to kill Duncan. Having done so, he regrets it immediately. Seeing his bloody hands, he says, *A sorry sight.* He is deeply disturbed by his inability to say *'Amen'*, as if guilt has cut him off from God.

In Act 3, scene 1, Macbeth attempts to justify his plan to murder Banquo. He thinks all will be well if he can just get rid of Banquo. He fears Banquo's *royalty of nature*, not only because Banquo might expose his crime, but because Banquo's virtue presents a constant contrast to his own sin.

✪ Would Macbeth be happy if he could somehow be sure of not being found out?

Imagination

Macbeth is more influenced by his imagination than most soldiers would be. When he first thinks of murder, he pictures it as a *horrid image* and speaks of his *horrible imaginings.* He also has the imagination to consider the consequences of the murder.

Before murdering Duncan, he imagines a dagger hovering before him. Afterwards he imagines a voice crying *Sleep no more!* In the banquet scene, only he sees Banquo's ghost. Is he just imagining it? Lady Macbeth certainly thinks so. She dismisses it as *the very painting of your fear*, comparing it to the *air-drawn dagger.* To her, imagination and fear are almost the same thing.

Monster or victim?

At the beginning of the play, Macbeth is highly praised, but by the end no one has a good word to say about him. ✪ Can his deeds be justified?

A link between Macbeth and the Witches is established in the opening scene, and it is Macbeth, not Banquo, whom they choose to lead astray by ambiguous promises. ✪ Why do you think they focus on him rather than Banquo? Would he have thought of murdering Duncan if he'd never met them?

✪ On the other hand, why does he think that he has to commit murder for the Witches' prophecy to come true? Duncan appoints Malcolm as his successor, but is this really an obstacle to the fulfilment of the prophecy?

We know that Macbeth is ambitious. He is clearly excited by the Witches' prophecy, and pleased to be made Thane of Cawdor. Later he says he has to kill Banquo and Fleance because otherwise Banquo's descendants will be kings, not his. He is ambitious for his own descendants – although as yet he has no children.

○ Look closely at Lady Macbeth's role. Does she just tell Macbeth what he wants to hear, and give him the courage to fulfil his ambitions? Or is she even more guilty than him?

How he changes

The first sign of Macbeth's dishonesty is when he pretends to Banquo that he has not been thinking about the Witches (Act 2, scene 1, line 21): *I think not of them.* After this, he becomes increasingly devious. He puts on a show of grief when Duncan's murder is discovered. He makes an apparently innocent enquiry about Banquo's plans for the afternoon in order to have him murdered. He keeps spies in every household.

Macbeth's decision to kill Banquo is a turning point. Up until this he has been bullied into action by his wife. But although he hints at his new plan to her, he keeps her *innocent of the knowledge.* He is becoming independent of her.

Another turning point is when at the end of the banquet scene Macbeth realises that there is now no going back:

> *I am in blood*
> *Stepp'd in so far, that, should I wade no more,*
> *Returning were as tedious as go o'er.*

Then there is the point where he is told by the Witches to be *bloody, bold and resolute,* and quickly decides to give up thinking before acting. He starts as he intends to go on, by resolving to wipe out Macduff's family.

In Act 5 we see Macbeth at first still clinging to the Witches' assurances that he cannot be beaten. When he realises that he's been tricked, and when his wife dies, he begins to despair. However, his pride won't let him surrender. Disillusioned and friendless, he fights fearlessly to the bitter end.

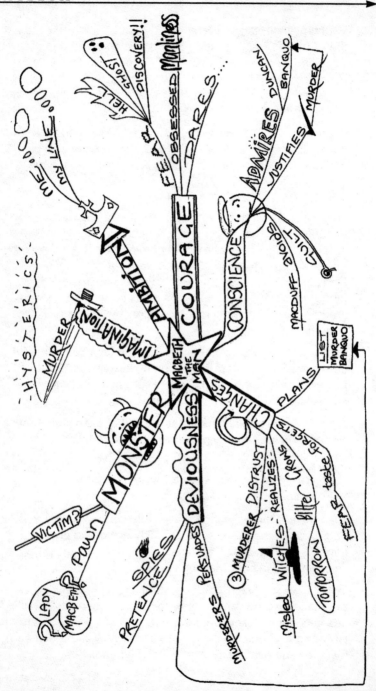

Test yourself

? Look back at the questions at the beginning of the section. Make brief notes in answer to them. Your opinions are perfectly valid if you can back them up with examples or quotations

now take a break before reading about Macbeth's 'fiend-like Queen'

Lady Macbeth

Questions to consider about Lady Macbeth:

◆ Is she a good wife?
◆ Is she possessed by evil?
◆ Does she bully her husband?
◆ Do you feel sorry for her when she dies?

A *woman possessed?*

Lady Macbeth makes her first appearance alone on stage in Act 1, scene 5, reading Macbeth's letter about the Witches. She believes instantly in the prophecy and assumes even more quickly than Macbeth that Duncan must be murdered for it to come true. Her only worry is that her husband may be *too full o' the milk of human kindness* to do the deed. She sees this as a weakness.

Shortly after this comes her blood-curdling *unsex me here* speech. She is determined that Duncan will die, and in order to prepare herself for her role, she appeals to the spirits of evil to fill her with *direst cruelty*, so that no womanly tenderness will soften her determination.

Despite her strength of will, she still needs a drink to help her with her part in Duncan's murder. She says that she would have killed him herself had he not reminded her of her father. ✪ Is this womanly tenderness, or just an excuse?

13

Her denial of reality

At the end of the *unsex me here* speech, we see a hint of the denial of reality that will eventually drive her mad. She appeals to night to *shroud* (cover) the coming murder in the darkest smoke of hell, so that even the knife cannot see the wound it makes, and so that heaven cannot *peep through the blanket of the dark.*

She has the same approach to Macbeth's hysteria after the murder: *Consider it not so deeply,* and *These deeds must not be thought/ after these ways; so, it will make us mad.* ✪ Is it possible to put aside guilt feelings in the way she recommends?

Her methods

When Macbeth decides not to kill Duncan, she calls him a coward. ✪ Is she deliberately playing on his insecurity? In another chilling speech (Act 1, scene 7), she says that she would have dashed her own baby's brains out if she had sworn to do so as Macbeth has sworn to kill Duncan. (Perhaps Shakespeare slipped up here, as she is childless – though she might have had children who died young.) This shows her ruthless determination. It also shows her manipulativeness: in fact Macbeth hasn't sworn to murder Duncan at all – he's only considered it.

✪ Is she being devious here? And what about her fainting after the discovery of Duncan's murder? Is it a trick to draw attention away from her husband? She certainly does her best to cover for him in the scene with Banquo's ghost.

Imagination and madness

She has no patience with Macbeth's fears, seeing them as childish imaginings. Some critics say that this is because she herself lacks imagination. When Macbeth speaks as if in a dream of *Sleep that knits up the ravell'd sleeve of care,* she answers only, *What do you mean?* To her, *A little water clears us of this deed.* This turns out to be far from true – as her obsessive hand-washing ritual while sleep-walking shows (Act 5, scene 1).

Her way of coping is to deny reality and to rely on her strength of will, but in the end the awful truth forces itself out through her unconscious, and even her will to live fails her. She becomes a broken woman, almost a girl again, complaining pathetically that *all the perfumes of Arabia will not sweeten this little hand.* ✪ Is her suicide an indication of her strength and self-reliance, or is it the final collapse of her character?

Now try this

?   Which of the following words describe Lady Macbeth?
     cruel   **feminine**   **loyal**   **ambitious**
         kind   **strong-willed**   **honest**
     Think of at least one piece of evidence for each choice.

?   Make a Mind Map of Lady Macbeth like the one for Macbeth on p. 12.

now that you've considerd what kind of woman Macbeth is married to, it's time for Mr Nice Guy – after the break!

Banquo

◆ Just how innocent is he?

Mr Nice Guy

We first see Banquo as Macbeth's equal in courage and action. Yet whereas Duncan rewards Macbeth with the title 'Thane of Cawdor', Banquo's only reward is praise. Some men would be envious, but not the noble Banquo. Again, the Witches do not set him on a path of murderous ambition, as they do Macbeth. He does not even take them very seriously at first – unlike Macbeth. As he says himself, he neither begs their favours nor fears their hate.

Macbeth himself speaks of Banquo's *royalty of nature*, the *dauntless temper of his mind,* and the *wisdom that doth guide his valour* (Act 3, scene 1, lines 50–3). He even finds time to take his son riding. So far he seems the kind of man any Scottish noble would want his daughter to marry. But is he?

The fall from grace

Banquo is unimpressed by the Witches, but they do predict that he will father kings. He is wary, and warns Macbeth against them (Act 1, scene 3, lines 122–6). In Act 2, scene 1, we find Banquo losing sleep over *cursed thoughts*. What might these be? When Macbeth wants to discuss the Witches again, he agrees – on the condition that he remains guilt-free.

So far Banquo has done nothing wrong. But then we hear his short soliloquy at the start of Act 3, scene 1, in which he expresses his fear that Macbeth *play'dst most foully* to get what the Witches promised. Yet in the same breath he hopes to benefit from their prophecy himself.

✪ Does Banquo do anything about his fears of foul play? Perhaps the answer is in his symbolic line, *I must become a borrower of the night.* In this play, night is associated with evil. Banquo is not evil, but by keeping quiet about the Witches and his suspicions about Macbeth he becomes tainted with evil. He becomes *a borrower of the night.*

Macduff

◆ What does he have in common with Macbeth?
◆ Why does he abandon his family?

A *simple man*

Macduff is a straightforward, sturdy, pleasant sort of man. He humours the Porter in Act 2, scene 3, listening patiently to his jokes. Then, when he discovers Duncan's murder, he is appalled and calls everyone to action.

Macbeth's insincere-sounding announcement of Duncan's death contrasts with Macduff's simple words: *Your royal father's murder'd.* Another contrast comes at the start of Act 4, scene 3, when Malcolm suggests they go and find somewhere to cry, and Macduff says, *Let us rather/ Hold fast the mortal sword.* He is a man of action – like Macbeth.

Macduff is also a man who shows strong feelings. Look at his response to Duncan's murder (Act 2, scene 3) and to the news of his own family's deaths (Act 4, scene 3).

Macduff's big mistake

Macduff does not go to Macbeth's coronation. This may be because he suspects Macbeth. However, it is harder to explain why he leaves his family unprotected when he goes to England to seek help against Macbeth. His wife cannot understand it. Couldn't he have sent a messenger, or left men to guard his castle? Malcolm wonders if the reason is that Macduff was on Macbeth's side and therefore felt safe. ❂ What do you think?

The loyalty test

Macduff is taken in by Malcolm's strange test of loyalty (Act 4, scene 3), in which he pretends to be unfit to be king. Macduff's bitter response – that Malcolm is unfit to live – proves his loyalty to Scotland. Shortly after this comes the moving scene in which Macduff hears of his family's massacre. He breaks down, blaming himself, but quickly resolves to avenge them – which he does by challenging and killing Macbeth in the final scene.

Ask yourself

? Who is the better man, Banquo or Macduff? Compare their strengths and weaknesses. If revising with a partner, take on the role of one character and defend him.

take a break before meeting Macbeth's first murder victim

Duncan

In the number of lines he speaks, Duncan is a minor character, but his role in the play is clearly central. As King, he is the head of the social order which his murder throws into chaos.

Duncan is too old to fight in battles, but he appreciates the efforts of Macbeth and Banquo. He thanks them graciously with tears of joy in his eyes, and he rewards Macbeth. He generously give Lady Macbeth a diamond in thanks for her hospitality. Macbeth himself sings his praises in the opening to Act 1, scene 7.

Malcolm

Malcolm is portrayed in more depth than Duncan. Yet, like Duncan, he is more important as a figurehead than as a realistic character.

✪ Why does Malcolm decide to flee when Duncan's murder is discovered? Isn't it obvious that this will make people suspect him and his brother Donalbain?

When Malcolm returns to Scotland, and to the play, he has learned not to trust too easily. He tests Macduff's loyalty by pretending to be an even worse man than Macbeth – and then admits that actually he's never done anything wrong in his life.

In the final speech of the play, Malcolm does what a king is supposed to do – he restores the social order.

Minor characters

The plot of *Macbeth* is simpler than most other Shakespeare plots, and so the only fully rounded characters are Macbeth and Lady Macbeth.

Lady Macduff is probably the most interesting minor character, in that she provides a contrast to Lady Macbeth.

The nobles Lennox, Ross, Menteith, Angus and Caithness all turn against Macbeth. Ross is the most important, as he brings information and comments on events, but he has no clearly defined character.

One slight mystery is the disappearance of Malcolm's younger brother Donalbain from the story after he has fled to Ireland. Perhaps the explanation is simply that he is no longer necessary to the plot.

As for the Witches, they are important, but they are personifications of evil rather than characters.

Test yourself

? Malcolm's list of *king-becoming graces* (Act 4, scene 3, lines 91–4) is shown below. Check that you know what each one means. Then number them in your own order of importance. What evidence of each grace can you see in Duncan and Malcolm?

> ... *justice, verity, temperance, stableness,*
> *Bounty, perseverance, mercy, lowliness,*
> *Devotion, patience, courage, fortitude.*

? List the minor characters from memory. Add a note on each one saying what their function is in the play.

? Look at the speeches of Ross, Lennox and Angus in Act 1, scenes 2–3. Do they have any individuality? Apply the same test to Act 5, scene 2.

? Each line below is spoken by one of the six main characters. Who says which line? How does each quote reflect the character who says it?

A. *Bleed, bleed, poor country*
B. *A little water clears us of this deed.*
C. *But wherefore could I not pronounce 'Amen'?*
D. *Angels are bright still, though the brightest fell.*
E. *Dispute it like a man.*
F. *More is thy due than more than all can pay.*
G. *The castle of Macduff I will surprise.*
H. *What, can the devil speak true?*
I. *Turn, hell-hound, turn!*
J. *unsex me here.*
K. *A heavy summons lies like lead upon me.*
L. *So well thy words become thee as thy wounds.*

ANSWERS:
Macbeth: C, G
Lady Macbeth: B, J
Duncan: F, L
Malcolm: D, E
Banquo: H, K
Macduff: A, I

by now you should be familiar with the characters in Macbeth. Take a break before tackling 'Themes and Imagery'

THEMES AND IMAGERY

A **theme** is an idea explored by an author. **Imagery** refers to the kind of word picture used to make that idea come alive.

Disorder

The importance of order

The idea of order was important in Shakespeare's time. It was thought that God had brought order to the universe, and that kings were appointed by God to preserve the social order and to be the head of that order themselves. How much have things changed?

Treachery and murder

The storm with which *Macbeth* opens reflects the disorder that the traitor Macdonwald has set in motion by rebelling against the King. The Witches' line, *Fair is foul, and foul is fair* applies both to the weather and to the country's disorder. Macbeth is identified with the Witches and with disorder by his similar line: *So foul and fair a day I have not seen.* ✪ Why was it fair for him?

Macbeth's murder of Duncan is a terrible crime, because it destroys the social order. It is a crime against God and nature.

In addition, because Macbeth is Duncan's host and relative, it is a crime against hospitality and family values.

For the social order to hold, men must be loyal to their superiors and to their country, and women must be loyal to their husbands. So loyalty is an important aspect of order – one which Malcolm focuses on in Act 4, scene 3, when he puts Macduff's loyalty to the test.

Imagery

There are images of disorder throughout the play. In Act 2, scene 3, Lennox reports that *The night has been unruly*. Strange screams and prophecies have been heard. When Macduff discovers Duncan dead he cries, *Confusion now hath made his masterpiece!*

In the next scene, Ross and an Old Man discuss how nature seems to be reflecting the awful event. Night and day are confused, an owl has killed a falcon, and of Duncan's horses, *'Tis said they ate each other*. This is echoed in Act 5, scene 1, by the Doctor: *Unnatural deeds/ Do breed unnatural troubles*. Whose disordered mind is he speaking about?

When Macbeth plans to murder Banquo, he speaks of cancelling a bond – a contract, suggesting the destruction of law and order. After the banquet at which Banquo's ghost appears, the guests leave in disorder, not according to rank.

Order restored

Malcolm's first act as king is to make his *thanes and kinsmen* earls, reinforcing the social order. He also promises to restore exiled friends and punish wrong-doers. In other words, order has returned to Scotland.

Sickness and health

The good kings Duncan and Malcolm are associated with health and growth – of individuals and the state. In Act 1, scene 4, Duncan promises Macbeth: *I have begun to plant thee, and will labour/ To make thee full of growing*. Malcolm uses a similar image in the final speech of the play. In Act 4, scene 3, we hear of King Edward's power to cure those suffering from *the Evil*, a form of tuberculosis.

Macbeth, on the other hand, brings sickness to his country – a sickness which he eventually acknowledges. In Act 5, scene 4, when the Doctor cannot cure Lady Macbeth, Macbeth exclaims impatiently, *Throw physic to the dogs; I'll none of it.* Then with grim irony he invites the Doctor to diagnose and cure Scotland's disease.

❂ Is Macbeth the cause of the sickness or a symptom?

The Supernatural

The supernatural is a powerful force in *Macbeth*, closely bound up with disorder.

Witches and spirits

The Witches, together with the moon goddess Hecate, are the main expression of the supernatural. They are evil incarnate: spiteful, destructive and deceptive. They trick Macbeth with half-truths rather than lies.

Shakespeare's audience would have taken witches and evil spirits very seriously, so when Lady Macbeth calls on spirits to fill her with cruelty in Act 1, scene 5, this would be seen as a real invitation to spirits to possess her. The *damned spot* she tries to wash off in her sleep would be seen as the mark of the devil. ❂ Does she seem to you to be possessed?

Banquo's ghost

Banquo's ghost is another example of the supernatural. Nowadays we might be inclined to see the ghost as a product of Macbeth's imagination, but Shakespeare's audience might have taken it more literally, even though only Macbeth can see it. ❂ What's your interpretation?

Prediction

In *Act 4, scene 1*, Macbeth commands the Witches to reveal the future. In response they show him a series of spirit apparitions which trick him into believing that he is indestructible.

Shakespeare cannot have felt that prediction was always evil, as the good King Edward is said, in Act 4, scene 3, to have *a heavenly gift of prophecy.*

Blood

Images of blood occur often in the play. We hear that Macbeth's sword *smoked with bloody execution,* there is the blood on his hands after Duncan's murder, and Macbeth describes Duncan as the fountain of his sons' blood. Blood can also suggest guilt, as when Lady Macbeth is distressed by the imaginary spot of blood on her hand that she cannot remove.

The supernatural significance of blood is seen in Macbeth's line after the appearance of Banquo's ghost: *It will have blood, they say; blood will have blood.*

Light and dark

Shakespeare uses light and dark as metaphors for good and evil, usually in the form of day and night. Macbeth is a creature of the night, who brings darkness to the land, but this cannot last for ever. As Malcolm says (Act 4, scene 3): *The night is long that never finds the day.*

The murders

Lady Macbeth calls on night to hide Duncan's murder *in the dunnest smoke of hell,* so that heaven does not *peep through the blanket of the dark.* (The night sky is seen as a blanket, with the stars as the light of heaven shining through its holes.)

The murder is committed on a starless night and discovered by day. Afterwards the Old Man tells Ross that darkness is strangling the sun. Banquo says he must become *a borrower of the night,* and he is murdered under cover of darkness.

The twilight world

The conflict between good and evil is seen most clearly at twilight, when day and night hang in the balance. One such time comes at the end of the banquet scene, when Lady Macbeth says the night is *Almost at odds with morning, which is which.* Another is at the end of Act 3, scene 2, when

Macbeth calls on night to *scarf up the tender eye of pitiful day.* He means that there must be no tenderness or pity. He goes on to paint a powerful picture of nightfall: *Light thickens, and the crow/ Makes wing to the rooky wood.*

Lady Macbeth

In madness, Lady Macbeth becomes afraid of the dark and always keeps a candle by her. ◎ What does this tell us about her?

Appearances

In this play appearances are deceptive. Things cannot be taken at face value. The Witches are women but have beards. *Fair is foul and foul is fair.* As Macbeth says in Act 1, scene 3, *nothing is/ But what is not.*

Macbeth and the Witches

At the heart of this deception are the Witches, who use *equivocation* (ambiguous, misleading words) to fool Macbeth. Macbeth's first lie is to deny to Banquo that he's been thinking about the Witches. He grows in dishonesty, acting out a show of grief over Duncan's death, making an apparently innocent enquiry in order to find out when he can have Banquo murdered, and giving the murderers false reasons for hating Banquo.

Lady Macbeth

In Act 1, scene 5, Lady Macbeth urges her husband to *look like the innocent flower/ But be the serpent under't.* In the banquet scene she desperately pretends to the guests that Macbeth is ill.

Malcolm

It is a sign of Malcolm's fitness to be king that he is less trusting than his father. He is aware of the *daggers in men's smiles* (Act 2, scene 3). He is also prepared to use deception himself – in a good cause. He tests Macduff's loyalty by pretending to be unfit to be king (Act 4, scene 3). He also tricks Macbeth by getting his men to disguise themselves as a wood.

Clothing imagery

Throughout the play there are images of clothing, a further suggestion that a man's appearance may not reflect what he is like inside.

Macbeth is reported to have *unseam'd* the traitor Macdonwald (like a tailor). Then when Macbeth is first called Thane of Cawdor (by Angus in Act 1, scene 3) he asks, *why do you dress me in borrow'd robes?* He doesn't realise that the old Thane of Cawdor has been stripped of his title.

Eventually, Macbeth is seen as a dwarf wearing a giant's clothes. He is king in name, but in reality he is unworthy of that title. ❂ Does he seem more comfortable once he is back in his armour at the end of the play?

Courage

Brave Macbeth

Macbeth is less honest and less noble than Banquo, but equally brave. Yet could there be a weakness behind Macbeth's courage? He is very sensitive to his wife's taunts about his manhood. Her accusations of cowardice persuade him to murder Duncan. Then when he is too afraid to take the daggers back to Duncan's chamber, she calls him *Infirm of purpose* and childish. She tells him she would be ashamed to *wear a heart so white* (so cowardly).

When Macbeth is terrified of Banquo's ghost, his wife asks, *Are you a man?* and *What! quite unmann'd in folly?* He tells the ghost that if it would only take the shape of a wild animal, he would fight it without fear – and that if he's not as good as his word, the ghost can call him *The baby of a girl.* ❂ Does it sound as if he's afraid of fear or of being thought unmanly?

Later he says he has *almost forgot the taste of fears*, and he dies fighting in proud defiance. Does this earn our respect? How do you feel when he taunts the *lily-liver'd boy* who brings news of the English army at the beginning of Act 5, scene 3?

Men, women and children

○ What other examples of courage can you think of in the play?

Macduff is clearly brave, and so is Young Siward, whose father wants to be reassured that his son has his wounds on the front of his body, showing that he was not running away.
○ What about Malcolm, who flees from Dunsinane after his father's murder?

Lady Macduff reacts bravely to the news that her life is in danger, and to the murderers who burst in. Her young son dies bravely, too.

○ Would you call Lady Macbeth brave? She is certainly strong-willed. Is her suicide a courageous act? What might have happened to her if she'd been captured?

Bring out the beast

Part of the theme of courage is the question of what makes a human being. In an important speech, Macbeth tells his wife:

I dare do all that may become a man;
Who dares do more, is none. (Act 1, scene 7, lines 46-7)

He means that a murderer has the same lack of moral scruples as an animal. Lady Macbeth takes up this idea and asks what *beast* made him suggest it to her in the first place.

The rest of the play is full of animal imagery, especially relating to Macbeth. Despite his intentions he becomes a beast. He refers to Banquo as a snake and says his own mind is *full of scorpions*. ○ What kind of animals are these? What similar images can you find in this scene (Act 3, scene 2)?

Macduff refers to Macbeth as a *hell-kite* (a kite is a bird of prey) that has killed his *pretty chickens* (his children). When he finally challenges Macbeth he calls him *hell-hound*. Macbeth in the end sees himself as a bear tied to a stake.

Sleep

This theme has several layers of meaning. It can suggest ignorance or lack of awareness: Duncan is murdered in his sleep, and Macduff has to wake everyone to report it next morning. It is also rather like death: Macbeth eventually envies Duncan the peaceful *sleep* of the dead.

When Macbeth murders Duncan he hears a voice crying, *Sleep no more!/ Macbeth does murder sleep*. In his hysteria he speaks longingly of *Sleep that knits up the ravell'd sleave of care*. Indeed, he and his wife never again have a good night's sleep. They are too tormented by guilt and worry.

Time

Time appears in the play many forms. ✪ Think for a moment about what time is. How would you explain it to someone with no understanding of it?

The future

Shakespeare explores the nature of time, starting with the Witches. They seem to see into the future, but by predicting it to Macbeth they become part of the process by which it happens. ✪ Would he have become king if he'd never met them? Would he have become king if he'd met them but not murdered Duncan?

Macbeth becomes obsessed with the future. He clearly thinks it can be predicted. ✪ Do you?

Troubled times

Time is also used in the sense of the troubled times in which the play is set. The strange occurrences in nature discussed by Ross and the Old Man are part of the mood of the time, as are battles, treachery and murder. When Macduff enters with Macbeth's head, he says that now *the time is free*, as if time itself has somehow been held captive by Macbeth.

The right moment

There is a sense in the play of things happening when they are meant to happen. In Act 4, scene 1, the Witches seem to be meeting at a precise moment, perhaps of magical importance: *'Tis time, 'tis time*. Banquo seems unwittingly to predict his own death: *our time does call upon's* (Act 3, scene 1). At the end of the play, Malcolm promises to do things *in measure, time, and place* in the correct order, at the right time, and in the proper place.

Eternity

Macbeth is aware that time marches on: *Come what may,/ Time and the hour runs through the roughest day.* He is also keenly aware of eternity. He knows that in murdering Duncan he has lost his *immortal soul.* He also speaks of life as a sandbank in the sea of eternity: *this bank and shoal of time* (Act 1, scene 7).

Seeing the vision of Banquo's descendants, he cries: *What! will the line stretch out to the crack of doom?* (He means the dawn of the end of time – Doomsday.) When his wife dies he despairingly pictures the days creeping on endlessly without meaning: *Tomorrow, and tomorrow, and tomorrow.*

Test yourself

? Now look at the complete Mind Map of themes on page 30, then close your book and see if you can make your own using colour, pictures and symbols. If you get stuck, look back at the incomplete Mind Map at the beginning of this chapter to start you off.

when you think you've understood and memorised the main themes in Macbeth, take a break before beginning the 'Commentary' chapter

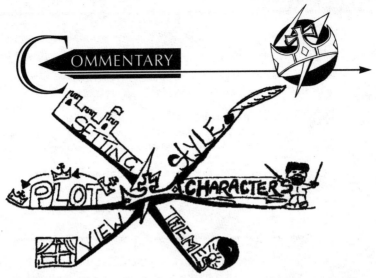

OMMENTARY

SETTING
STYLE
PLOT
CHARACTERS
VIEW
THEME

The Commentary looks at each scene in turn, beginning with a brief preview which will prepare you for the scene and help in last-minute revision. The Commentary comments on whatever is important in the scene, focusing on the areas shown in the Mini Mind Map above.

Wherever there is a focus on a particular theme, the icon for that theme appears in the margin (see p. 10 for key). Look out, too, for the 'Style and language' sections. Being able to comment on style and language will help you to get an 'A' in your exam.

You will learn more from the Commentary if you use it alongside the play itself. Read a scene from the play, then the corresponding Commentary section – or the other way round.

Remember that when a question appears in the Commentary with a star ✪ in front of it, you should stop and think about it for a moment. And remember to take a break after completing each exercise!

Act 1 *scene* 1

◆ Mood set.
◆ Witches agree to meet again, with Macbeth.

The play begins with thunder and lightning, on a moor (or heath). This catches the audience's attention and sets the mood of the play. To Shakespeare's audience, a moor would have seemed a wild, lonely and frightening place – especially in foul weather.

We first hear of Macbeth from the 3rd Witch. This links him with the Witches. ◑ What does this suggest about him?

 The line *Fair is foul, and foul is fair* is important. It suggests that things have been turned upside down, and that appearances, whether of good or evil, cannot be trusted.

The rhythm and rhyme of the Witches' lines sound as if they are chanting a spell. Try reading them aloud.

Act 1 *scene* 2

◆ Sergeant brings news of victory achieved by Macbeth and Banquo against the traitor Macdonwald and the Norwegians.
◆ We meet King Duncan and his sons Malcolm and Donalbain; also Lennox and Ross.
◆ Ross reports a further victory, against the Thane of Cawdor and the Norwegians.
◆ Macbeth and Banquo seen as loyal, courageous fighters, Duncan as quick to reward virtue and punish villainy.

This scene tells us what has been happening before the start of the play. Macbeth and Banquo have led Duncan's army to victory against Macdonwald, the Thane of Cawdor, and the Norwegians. Shakespeare uses the Sergeant (sometimes called the Captain) to tell the first part of the story, and Ross the second. ◑ Why do you think Shakespeare does this, rather than staging the battle?

How *the story is told*

The Sergeant keeps up the suspense by letting the story out bit by bit.

He describes the uncertainty of the battle, and the courage of Macbeth and Banquo, who were no more dismayed by the enemy than eagles are by sparrows, or lions by hares (line 35). The story is completed by Ross. He says he has just come from Fife. Geographically, this is confusing, as Fife is a hundred miles from Forres, which is where this scene is set. Either Shakespeare slipped up here, or he is running two battles into one for the sake of the story.

Duncan rewards Macbeth by making him the new Thane of
Cawdor.

The play often combines images of blood and water.
Ironically, it is Duncan who first mentions blood (line 1).
The Sergeant describes the two exhausted armies as being like
two spent swimmers (line 8). He also wonders whether
Macbeth and Banquo meant to bathe in blood (line 40).

The Sergeant tells his story. Who to? Who else is listening? What news does he bring?

The Sergeant's description uses three important literary devices
that you should try to understand, memorise, and look out for:

1 A **simile** compares two things which are different in most
ways but similar in one important way. His likening of the
armies to swimmers is a simile.

2 A **metaphor** speaks of one thing as if it is something else. Again, there must be a basic difference, but also a similarity. The Sergeant says that Macbeth *unseam'd* Macdonwald – as if Macdonwald is an item of clothing being ripped apart at the seam.

3 A **personification** speaks of something abstract as if it is a person. The Sergeant describes fortune as a woman smiling on Macdonwald.

Act 1 *scene* 3

◆ Sailor's wife story.
◆ Witches predict future for Macbeth and Banquo.
◆ Ross and Angus bring word from Duncan.
◆ Macbeth and Banquo react to news that one prediction has come true.

The sailor's wife

The scene again begins with thunder, on the moor. The 1st Witch tells how a sailor's wife refused to give her any chestnuts.

The 1st Witch plans to punish the wife by tormenting the sailor with storms and lack of sleep (lines 19–20). This shows the Witches' spiteful nature.

The Witches predict

We meet Macbeth and Banquo for the first time. Macbeth's opening line is significant: *So foul and fair a day I have not seen.*

This echoes the Witches' earlier words, linking Macbeth with them. It also plays on the theme of disorder. What is *foul* (battle) is also *fair* (victory).

The Witches predict that Macbeth will be King and Banquo will father kings. Banquo is suspicious of the Witches. However, he is unafraid, probably because he is a good man and therefore they have no power over him. He notices that Macbeth is startled (line 51).

He comments to the Witches that Macbeth is *rapt withal.* This is a **pun**, a use of a word with two meanings, or of two similar-sounding words, where both meanings are appropriate in different ways: Macbeth is *rapt*, meaning amazed, and *wrapped*, as in a cloak or other garment.

Word from Duncan

Ross and Angus come to thank Macbeth, fetch him back to Duncan, and tell him that he is now Thane of Cawdor. Macbeth at first fails to understand. He asks *why do you dress me/ In borrow'd robes?* We see here the clothing image again. Soon Macbeth will be wearing what he does not deserve, the *borrow'd robes* of a king.

Macbeth and Banquo react

 Banquo suspects the Witches. He says, *... oftentimes, to win us to our harm,/ The instruments of darkness tell us truths.* Even truth can be a means of trickery.

Macbeth is deeply disturbed. In his first **soliloquy** (a speech delivered by a character alone on stage as if thinking aloud), he finds himself thinking of murder. The idea is only in his imagination (*fantastical*), yet it shakes him to the core. The thought of what it might bring paralyses him (lines 139–41), although it then occurs to him that chance may make him king without his having to do anything (*without my stir*). ❂ What do you think he should do?

Banquo again says that Macbeth is *rapt* and comments that Macbeth, with his new title, is like a man wearing *strange garments* which will only fit comfortably with time.

Test yourself

? Macbeth and Banquo are both brave fighters, but in what ways do they differ? Make a list or Mind Map.

? What role has the weather played in the play so far?

? Look back at Macbeth's **asides** (lines spoken by one character, as if thinking aloud, not meant to be heard by other characters on stage). What do these lines tell us about him?

? Compare Macbeth's soliloquy with his words to the others in the speech beginning, *Give me your favour* (scene 3, lines 149–55). What impression does he want to create?

Act 1 *scene* 4

♦ Thane of Cawdor's execution reported.
♦ Duncan thanks Macbeth and Banquo.
♦ Duncan announces that Malcolm is heir to throne.

The scene is set in Duncan's palace. Duncan asks if the treacherous Thane of Cawdor has been executed yet. Malcolm says that he has.

He adds that although he was a traitor he died bravely: *Nothing in his life/ Became him like the leaving it.*
Duncan comments that he had trusted this man, and that it shows there's no way to tell someone's real character from their face. This is an ironic warning to the audience, since Duncan trusts Macbeth, calling him *worthiest cousin*. In fact, by the end of the scene Macbeth is already thinking of murdering Duncan. ✪ What does the new Thane of Cawdor have in common with the old one?

Duncan speaks of Macbeth as if he is a plant that he intends to *make ... full of growing.* Banquo politely takes up this metaphor, saying that if he grows in Duncan's heart, the harvest will be Duncan's. When Malcolm becomes King at the end of the play, he uses the same metaphor.

Duncan names Malcolm *Prince of Cumberland* (rather like 'Prince of Wales'), meaning that he has chosen Malcolm to inherit the throne. Macbeth thinks this presents an obstacle to his becoming king himself.

Macbeth's ambition

By the end of the scene Macbeth is seriously considering murder. The line *Stars, hide your fires!* suggests the time for doing the deed. He does not want his eye to see what his hand does. ✪ Macbeth is ambitious, but how does he seem to feel about this idea developing in his mind?

Act 1 *scene* 5

◆ Lady Macbeth reads of Macbeth's successes, and of the Witches' promises.
◆ Messenger announces that Duncan is to stay at Macbeth's castle.
◆ Lady Macbeth immediately plans to murder Duncan.
◆ Macbeth returns home.

The scene takes place in Macbeth's castle. It begins with Lady Macbeth reading a letter from her husband about his meeting with the Witches. Although the letter does not suggest murder, Lady Macbeth assumes it is necessary. However, she fears that Macbeth is *too full o' the milk of human kindness* to do it. She sees this as a weakness which she must *chastise* out of him.
❂ What theatrical advantage is there in her receiving the news by letter?

Lady Macbeth is taken aback by the news that Duncan is coming. She has had no time to prepare. After the messenger has gone, she speaks a chilling soliloquy, in which she anticipates *the fatal entrance of Duncan/ under my battlements*, and calls on spirits to take away any trace of womanly pity that might prevent her from committing murder.
❂ How is the end of her speech like Macbeth's in the previous scene when he says, *The eye wink at the hand; yet let that be/ Which the eye fears, when it is done, to see?*

Read aloud Lady Macbeth's powerful soliloquy (lines 37–53), in which she calls up spirits – *murdering ministers*. ❂ What is the effect of the rhythm in the phrases *unsex me here* and *make thick my blood* and of the hard 'c' sounds of the words *crown, cruelty* and *compunctious*?

What do you associate with the croaking raven at the start of the speech? Ravens are black. What other images of darkness occur in this speech?

Heaven is personified at the end of the speech. ❂ Which sounds more powerful – heaven or hell?

Notice the image from nature that Lady Macbeth uses in her advice to her husband (lines 64–5): *look like the innocent flower/ But be the serpent under't.* You might like to draw this in your notes as a way of fixing it in your memory.

Act 1 *scene* 6

◆ Duncan and his party arrive at Macbeth's castle and are greeted by Lady Macbeth.

 In this short scene we see Duncan arrive at Macbeth's castle. It is ironic that Duncan finds it so pleasant, and that Banquo sees the presence of house martins (birds that nest on buildings) as a sign that the air here is healthy.

Lady Macbeth speaks to Duncan graciously and flatteringly. She is clearly a talented deceiver.

Act 1 *scene* 7

◆ Macbeth decides that he should not murder Duncan after all.
◆ He tells his wife this, and she calls him a coward. She persuades him to continue with their plan.

This important scene takes place in a room in Macbeth's castle. It comes in tense contrast to the relaxed, airy atmosphere of the previous scene at the castle gate.

*M*acbeth's big decision

Macbeth, thinking aloud, tries to make up his mind about murdering Duncan. At first, he speaks in the short, halting phrases of a man who is tense and cannot decide what to do. If the murder is to be done, then he wants to get it over and done with quickly.

 He knows that to kill a king is a terrible crime, punishable by eternal damnation. However, he says that if he could be sure that the crime would put a stop to (*trammel up*) further consequences, and succeed immediately, then he'd ignore the life to come. He sees life as a sandbank in the sea of eternity.

Macbeth considers five good reasons for not killing Duncan:

• They are related.
• He is Duncan's subject.

- He is Duncan's host.
- Duncan is a good man.
- Being over-ambitious could be his downfall, like a horse that attempts too high a jump (*o'er-leaps itself/ And falls ...*).

Notice how Macbeth uses clothing imagery in justifying his decision to his wife. He says he is now admired and respected. *He has ... bought/ Golden opinions from all sorts of people*, and he wants to wear them, like new clothes.

Lady Macbeth persuades

Lady Macbeth takes up the clothing image when she asks whether the hope in which he had *dress'd* himself had been drunk.

She calls him a coward, and says he is like the cat in the adage (proverb) that wants to eat fish but won't get its feet wet. ✪ In what way is this true of Macbeth?

Notice that she suggests that the murder plan (*enterprise*) was Macbeth's. ✪ Is this true? She goes on to say that she would kill her own baby if she had sworn to do it, as Macbeth has done to kill Duncan. In fact, the nearest Macbeth has come to committing himself so far is at the end of scene 5, when he says, *We will speak further.*

Lady Macbeth knows her husband well. As soon as he waivers in his resolve to go no further, and says, *If we should fail –*, she seizes her advantage. She spells out how they will commit the murder. By the end of the scene, Macbeth is convinced.

Compare the hesitant, uncertain tone and gentle imagery (*this bank and shoal of time*) of Macbeth's first speech with the strong rhythms and violent imagery of his wife's words. Notice the shocking switch from tender motherhood to violence when she says she would have *dash'd the brains out.* This also contrasts with Macbeth's image of *pity, like a naked new-born babe.*

Notice, too, the strong imagery and firm rhythm of: *But screw your courage to the sticking-place,/ And we'll not fail.* (This may refer to screwing up a tuning peg on a musical instrument, or to drawing a crossbow.)

Now try this

? Compare Macbeth and Lady Macbeth as shown in scenes 3–7. How do their words reflect their characters?

? Trace the key stages in Macbeth's decision-making, from where he first considers killing Duncan, at the end of scene 3, through his uncertainty and decision not to commit the crime, to his being persuaded. Draw this as a flow-chart or Mind Map. Include representative lines from his speeches in boxes.

tension's mounting, time for a break

Act 2 *scene* 1

◆ Banquo and his son Fleance meet Macbeth at night in the castle courtyard.

◆ Macbeth thinks aloud about the murder he's about to commit. Sees vision of dagger and goes to do the deed.

The scene is set in the courtyard of Macbeth's castle. It is past midnight, the moon has gone down, and there are no stars (*candles*) in the sky. Banquo doesn't want to go to bed, because he is afraid of *cursed thoughts*. His nervousness is shown by his *Give me my sword./ Who's there?*

Banquo says that Duncan has been enjoying himself. He shows, or gives, Macbeth a diamond which is a present from the King to his hostess, Lady Macbeth. ❂ What is a diamond like? In what way is it an appropriate gift for her?

Macbeth is lying when he says he hasn't thought about the Witches (*the three weird sisters*). He says that he would like to talk to Banquo about them when he has time. Banquo's reply, in which he says he wants to keep his heart free from guilt (*bosom franchis'd*), shows his suspicion.

'**I**s this a dagger which I see before me ...?'

Macbeth's *Is this a dagger ...* speech is worth reading carefully. Notice that it falls into three parts.

First, Macbeth speaks to the dagger he seems to see before him. He wonders if the vision comes from his feverish (*heat-oppressed*) brain. It seems to draw him towards murder. The blood on the blade and hilt (*dudgeon*) is as if the deed has already been done. With the words, *There's no such thing*, Macbeth decides that he is imagining things.

The second part of the speech draws us into the atmosphere of horror that goes with the awful crime that is about to be committed. In the half of the world where it is night, nature itself seems dead – and he is about to commit a crime that goes against nature. He imagines *wicked dreams*, witchcraft, and murder personified, accompanied by a howling wolf. He compares murder with the rape committed by the Roman Tarquin. His fearful imagination even makes him afraid that the stones on which he walks will speak out and give him away.

In the last part of the speech, Macbeth pulls himself together, realising that he must stop talking and get on with the murder. He hears the bell that is Lady Macbeth's signal. Then, with a rhyming couplet that seems to wrap up the speech, as if he has finally made up his mind, he goes into action.

Act 2 *scene* 2

◆ Macbeth and wife meet as soon as Macbeth has murdered Duncan.
◆ Macbeth is terrified by what he's done. Lady Macbeth tries to talk him out of his fears.
◆ Lady Macbeth returns the bloody daggers to Duncan's chamber.

This is a crucial scene. It begins with Lady Macbeth, who has had a drink to give herself courage. Despite this she is nervous and afraid that Macbeth has failed in the deed. She knows that *the attempt and not the deed* – unsuccessfully attempting the murder – would ruin them both.

Lady Macbeth says that she would have murdered Duncan herself if he had not reminded her of her own father. ❂ How does this compare with her fierce *unsex me here* speech in Act 1, scene 5, in which she calls on spirits to make her cruel?

The dialogue between Macbeth and his wife is at first composed of short, jerky phrases. ✪ What does this show about their mood?

Macbeth already regrets what he has done. He looks at his bloody hands and says, *This is a sorry sight.* Lady Macbeth says he's being foolish. Throughout the scene, Macbeth is tormented by his own terrified imagination, while his wife becomes calm and practical. She seems much more down to earth. Her method of coping with guilt is to avoid thinking about it. Otherwise, she says, *it will make us mad.*

Why do you think Macbeth is troubled by not being able to say *Amen* when he heard Malcolm and Donalbain saying their prayers?

'**S**leep that knits up the ravell'd sleave of care'

 Still almost beside himself, Macbeth tells his wife how he heard a voice crying, *Sleep no more!* She interrupts with a simple *What do you mean?*

She is less imaginative than him, and she takes his guilty conscience as a mere sign of cowardice. ✪ Is it?

The image of water as a means of washing away guilt is important here and elsewhere. When Lady Macbeth later goes mad, she repeatedly makes the action of washing her hands. Shakespeare's audience might see water as life-giving as well as cleansing. It is contrasted with the blood that flows so freely in the play.

Read Macbeth's speech beginning, *Whence is that knocking?* (line 57). He says that every sound *appals* him. Taken literally this means makes him pale, drains his blood. However, his hands are covered in Duncan's blood. The sight makes his eyes almost fall out of his head. He wonders if the whole ocean will wash them clean. The grandness of the words *multitudinous* and *incarnadine* (make red, as in *carn*ation) suggest the vastness of the sea and of the murder committed. These words contrast with the simplicity of the next line.

Compare Lady Macbeth's attitude in the next speech. She uses the image of water, but in a very different way: *A little water clears us of this deed.* In other words, all they have to do is wash their hands! ✪ Which seems more true to you?

Think about it

? In his *Is this a dagger ...* speech (scene 1), Macbeth seems horrified at the thought of murdering Duncan. Why in your opinion does he still do it?

? How does Lady Macbeth give herself courage (scene 2, line 1)?

? What, according to Lady Macbeth, stops her from killing Duncan (scene 2, lines 13–14)? What does this say about her character?

Act 2 *scene* 3

◆ Porter opens castle gates and jokes with Macduff and Lennox.
◆ We hear of strange things occurring the night before.
◆ Duncan's murder discovered. Macbeth kills Duncan's servants.
◆ Malcolm and Donalbain decide to flee.

The Porter

The scene begins with a continuation of the knocking at the castle gates which Macbeth has already been frightened by in *scene 2*. The Porter's reaction to it is very different from Macbeth's. He makes a joke of it, providing us with comic relief after the tension of the last scene. At the same time, there is **dramatic irony**. We know that while the Porter jokes about being the Porter of Hell's Gate, Duncan lies murdered. We also know that there really is something hellish about Dunsinane. (See p. 53 for more about **irony**.)

The Porter, as a lowly character, speaks in **prose** (ordinary, non-poetic sentences – like this one), not in **blank verse** (the kind of non-rhyming verse, with five pairs of syllables to each line, that most of the play is in). He jokingly imagines who it might be at the gate – a greedy farmer, an equivocator (someone who uses words to conceal the truth), or a dishonest tailor.

The Porter lets in Macduff and Lennox, and continues to joke. He says he was drinking until after dawn, and that drink gives a man a red nose, makes him sleepy, and makes him want to urinate. It makes him want sex but also makes him less capable of it.

Macbeth enters and talks to Lennox and Macduff. They ask if Duncan is due to leave the castle today, and Macbeth says he is. ✪ How do you think Macbeth feels during this conversation?

While Macduff goes to wake Duncan, Lennox reports strange and unnatural events that occurred during the previous night, including *strange screams of death*. Macbeth answers briefly: '*Twas a rough night*. ✪ Why was it particularly rough for him?

The discovery

Macduff rushes in with the news of Duncan's murder. He says that *Confusion now hath made his masterpiece!* Confusion is chaos, the opposite of order. Remember that order was especially important to Shakespeare's audience. The King heads the social order, and now he is dead.

Macduff is shocked and outraged, but he responds as a man of action. He orders the bell to be sounded to wake everyone up. ✪ Read his *Approach the chamber ...* speech (lines 72–81) aloud. Note its repetitions. How does it sound? Is it believable?

Lady Macbeth enters. Hearing that Duncan has been murdered, she responds inappropriately: *What! in our house?* The awful thing, after all, is that he's been murdered at all – not in whose house. Banquo notices this and comments, *Too cruel anywhere.*

Macbeth re-enters. His speech beginning *Had I but died an hour before this chance,/ I had liv'd a blessed time ...* (lines 92–7) sounds sincere. It is true that the best of his life is over, and that now only the *lees* (dregs) are left – even if those hearing him think that his sorrow is purely because Duncan is murdered, not because he is the murderer.

After this, Macbeth starts to sound less sincere, as he tries to impress everyone with his grief. Look at his exaggerated, fanciful imagery: *The spring, the head, the fountain of your blood/ Is stopp'd; the very source of it is stopp'd.* Compare this with Macduff's *Your royal father's murder'd.*

The cover-up

Macbeth sounds even less sincere when he attempts to justify his slaying of Duncan's servants. He claims he could not resist killing the murderers. In reality he has panicked and done this in case they are believed and he is found out.

Lady Macbeth pretends to faint in order to draw attention away from her husband. ❂ Do you think this works?

Duncan's sons fear treason and decide to flee the country.
❂ Is this the right decision? How will their flight be interpreted?

Act 2 *scene* 4

◆ Ross and Old Man discuss unnatural events of the night before.
◆ Macduff brings news that Duncan's sons have fled and are suspected of his murder, and that Macbeth has been chosen as king.

The first part of this short scene comments on the strange way in which nature seems to be echoing the terrible events in the human world. The events are worse than any the Old Man can remember. Ross says that although according to the clock it is day, darkness blots out the sun: *... dark night strangles the travelling lamp.* It seems that even the sun is being murdered.

The Old Man says that an owl has killed a hawk – which would never normally happen, and we hear that Duncan's horses have turned savage and attacked each other.

Macduff brings the news that Malcolm and Donalbain have fled and are suspected of murdering their father. He also says that Macbeth has been chosen as king.

Test yourself

? Why does the Porter take so long to come to the gate? Who does he let in? What effect do his jokes have on us?

? In scene 4 we hear that Duncan's horses have been behaving strangely. Who tells us? How is it significant?

now take a break before looking at Macbeth's next murder plan

Act 3 *scene* 1

◆ Banquo thinks about the Witches' predictions.
◆ Macbeth asks Banquo to come to a banquet. Banquo says he'll go riding with his son Fleance beforehand.
◆ Macbeth justifies his plan to kill Banquo and Fleance.
◆ Macbeth engages two murderers to kill Banquo and Fleance. He compares the murderers to dogs.

The scene is set in a room in the royal palace. It begins with a soliloquy from Banquo which is short but important for two reasons:

• We see Banquo clearly suspecting Macbeth of Duncan's murder.
• We learn that despite this, Banquo still hopes that the Witches' prophecies for him may come true.

Macbeth and Lady Macbeth make their entry, together with Lennox, Ross and others. Macbeth invites Banquo to a banquet, as the most honoured guest. Yet he is already plotting to murder Banquo. As if making conversation, he asks whether Banquo plans to go riding, and how far he plans to go. ✪ Why does he want to know?

Notice that Banquo says, *go not my horse the better,/ I must become a borrower of the night/ For a dark hour or twain*. He means that unless his horse goes especially fast, it will be dark an hour or two before he gets back. Remember that in this play darkness is connected to evil. Banquo is not a bad man, but he keeps quiet about his suspicions. He also hopes to benefit from the Witches' prophecies. ❂ If in this play *night* equals 'evil', what might be the deeper meaning of Banquo being a *borrower of the night*?

If you have read scene 4, the banquet scene, you may notice the irony when Macbeth says to Banquo, *Fail not our feast* (Don't miss it), and Banquo replies, *My lord, I will not.* ❂ Will he?

Justifying Banquo's murder

Once Banquo has gone, Macbeth sends for two murderers. While waiting for them to come, he speaks an important soliloquy, beginning ... *To be thus is nothing;/ But to be safely thus*. This means that being king is worthless unless the position is secure. He justifies the murder of Banquo and Fleance to himself, and to us, in two ways:

- Banquo is noble, brave and wise, and therefore to be feared because he might see through Macbeth and successfully oppose him.
- The Witches have prophesied that a line of kings will descend from Banquo, but not Macbeth. If so, then Macbeth has murdered Duncan for nothing.

Macbeth says that Banquo makes his spirit (his *genius*) timid, just as Caesar did Mark Antony's. What's more, the Witches have *put a barren sceptre* in Macbeth's grip. The sceptre is a sort of decorated rod held by a king. ❂ The word 'barren' here means childless, so what is Macbeth saying?

Macbeth feels deeply guilty about murdering *gracious* Duncan. If he had no conscience he would feel no *rancours* (bitterness). Worse, he knows that he has given his soul (his *eternal jewel*) to the devil (*the common enemy of man*).

Persuading the murderers

Macbeth is getting better at dishonesty. See how he persuades the murderers that they have reason to avenge themselves on Banquo. Do you remember how Lady Macbeth taunted Macbeth to murder Duncan by questioning his manhood? Macbeth now does something similar with the murderers. He asks if they are so patient and so Christian (*gospell'd*) that they will put up with what Banquo has done to them. When they answer that they are men, he continues to goad them. He says that they are of the species of men, just as all breeds of dog are dogs. He is really asking if they are *real* men.

The men say that they have suffered such misfortune that they are now desperate enough to try anything. Macbeth says that he'd order Banquo's death himself, but for the fact that they have friends in common. By the time he tells them *Resolve yourselves apart* (Go off and decide), their minds are made up.

Act 3 *scene* 2

◆ Macbeth shows signs of stress and anxiety.
◆ Lady Macbeth tries to reassure him.
◆ Macbeth hints that he is having Banquo murdered.

❂ What is the effect of beginning this scene (and many others) with a question? Lady Macbeth's question is probably an anxious one. Even though her husband is now king, she complains that *Nought's had, all's spent,/ Where our desire is got without content*. They've got what they wanted, but they're still not happy.

When Macbeth enters, she tries to persuade him to make the most of things. She says, *Things without all remedy/ Should be without regard*. This is another way of saying, *Don't worry about what you can't change.* ❂ Is this sound advice? What difference does it show between them?

Macbeth says that they are only part-way to achieving their goal: *We have scorch'd* [*wounded*] *the snake, not kill'd it.* Notice that this is another animal image. Later, in scene 4, he refers to Banquo as a serpent. In scene 2 (line 36) he complains that his mind is *full of scorpions*. ✪ What must he feel like to describe himself in this way?

 Macbeth seems almost envious of Duncan now: *After life's fitful fever he sleeps well.*

Lady Macbeth says that Banquo and Fleance are not immortal (*eterne*). ✪ Do you think she just means that they must die one day?

Using more animal imagery – the bat, the *shard-born beetle*, Macbeth hints at Banquo's murder. But he doesn't quite spell it out to his wife. He wants her to be *innocent of the knowledge* until the deed is done.

In an earlier speech he calls her *love*. Here he calls her *dearest chuck*. ✪ How do you think he feels about her? Does he keep her ignorant of his new murder plan to protect her?

 Scene 3 ends with a poetically powerful speech. Read from line 46: *Come, seeling night ...* This is one of the speeches in the play when a character appeals to an outer force. Lady Macbeth in Act 1, scene 5 appeals to evil spirits (*Come, you spirits*). Now Macbeth personifies night – or the forces of darkness – and asks it to blindfold the *tender eye of pitiful day*. There is no room for kindness, and it is better that dark deeds remain unseen.

Try to picture night's *bloody and invisible hand* moving through the darkness. The *great bond* which it must tear up could be the bond between Banquo's body and soul. A bond means a legal contract. ✪ Could it mean that Macbeth wants to destroy law itself?

Macbeth observes the gathering dusk: *Light thickens ....* It is as if light is a liquid that becomes harder to move through (or see through) as it thickens – like blood congealing. The approach of night is summed up in the image of the crow flying to the *rooky wood* (what colour are crows and rooks?). Good things begin to lose power, *Whiles night's black agents to their preys do rouse.* ✪ How would you feel out on your own on a night like this?

Act 3 *scene* 3

◆ The two murderers are joined by a third.
◆ They murder Banquo, but Fleance escapes.

 Macbeth trusts no one, so he has sent a third murderer to join the first two. Banquo and Fleance are returning from their ride. It is already dark, and Banquo calls for a light from the grooms who take charge of the horses. Banquo and Fleance, now on foot, appear on stage and are attacked. Fleance flees, and Banquo dies. ✪ What are Banquo's last words? To whom are they addressed?

Ask yourself

? Is Banquo completely innocent? If in doubt, look back to his speech at the beginning of *scene 1*.

? What do you understand by the word 'irony'? In what way is it ironic when Macbeth says to Banquo *Fail not our feast* and Banquo replies *My lord, I will not*?

? What animal imagery do you remember from the play so far? (There is a lot in *scene 2*.) Jot down (or sketch) the animals you remember. Next to each, write one word that comes to mind when you think of that animal.

Act 3 *scene* 4

◆ Macbeth and wife welcome guests to banquet.
◆ Murderer appears and tells Macbeth that Banquo is dead but that Fleance has escaped.
◆ Ghost of Banquo appears and terrifies Macbeth.
◆ Lady Macbeth tries to persuade guests that Macbeth's behaviour is normal for him. In the end she gives up and asks them to leave.

The scene centres on the banquet. The guests sit according to their *degrees* (status). Macbeth is trying to be a good host when one of the murderers arrives with news of Banquo's death. Macbeth is pleased at first, but deeply disappointed to hear that Fleance has escaped. With Fleance dead, he might have felt free *as the casing air*. Instead, he is feels *cabin'd, cribb'd, confin'd, bound in/ To saucy doubts and fears*. Notice the alliteration: the hard 'c' sounds reflect Macbeth's hopes of freedom being cut off.

Macbeth refers to Banquo as a serpent, and to Fleance as a worm. He tells himself that Fleance is not yet a threat.

Lady Macbeth reminds him that he is meant to be hosting a banquet. Then, just as he is saying what a pity it is that Banquo is missing, Banquo's ghost appears – but only to Macbeth.

All in the mind?

❂ How well do you think Lady Macbeth does in convincing the guests that all is well? Is she doing the right thing when she tries to make Macbeth pull himself together by questioning his manhood (*Are you a man?* and *What! quite unmann'd in folly?*)

The ghost goes, and Macbeth manages to pull himself together, even proposing a toast *to our dear friend Banquo*. But when the ghost returns, Macbeth falls apart again. He is terrified, but he insists that he is no coward (*What man dare, I dare*). He says he could deal with a bear, a rhinoceros or a tiger, but not with this *horrible shadow*.

The guests leave

Lady Macbeth accuses her husband of spoiling the party and drawing attention to himself. He wonders at her ability to remain calm.

The guests leave in hurried disorder, and the exhausted royal couple are alone. ✪ How must each feel now? It is almost dawn, that time popularly called 'the darkest hour'. Night is *at odds with morning*, suggesting the battle between good and evil. A new worry now comes to Macbeth: why has Macduff not come to the feast? We see further into his distrust and his style of kingship when he says that he will find out through his spies.

✪ Is it pity or exhaustion that makes Lady Macbeth speak so simply in her line, *You lack the season of all natures, sleep*?

The scene ends with a chilling warning that there is worse to come: *We are yet but young in deed*.

Act 3 *scene 5*

◆ Hecate meets with the Witches.

This scene is often cut, because it adds little to the story and because its rather wooden style is not typical of Shakespeare. It was probably added by a later writer to satisfy popular demand to see more of the Witches. Hecate, goddess of witchcraft and the moon, rebukes the Witches for dealing with Macbeth without her. She tells them to get ready for their next meeting with him.

✪ Does Hecate's speech sound like Shakespeare? Notice the rhyme scheme. In normal blank verse there are ten syllables: *You lack the season of all natures, sleep*. Tap out the rhythm. Then do the same with one of Hecate's lines: *To trade and traffic with Macbeth.* How many syllables are there? Try other lines.

Act 3 *scene* 6

◆ Lennox discusses recent events ironically with another lord.
◆ The lord brings news: Malcolm is a guest in the court of the English king, Edward; Macduff has gone there to ask for help in overthrowing Macbeth.

This scene takes place in the royal palace. It lets us know how the situation is developing, but nothing actually happens.

Read Lennox's opening speech. It is full of **irony**. In other words, Lennox says almost the opposite of what he really means, and yet his meaning is fairly clear to anyone with knowledge of the situation he is talking about. For example, he seems to say Banquo was to blame for his own death: *men must not walk too late.* ✪ And is it likely that young Fleance would have killed his own father?

The lord's news – that Malcolm is at the English court and that Macduff has gone to raise an army to fight Macbeth – prepares us for the action to come. ✪ What are the dramatic advantages of informing us like this, rather than having a scene showing Macduff at the English court?

 STYLE AND LANGUAGE

There are two types of irony in this play:
1 **Dramatic irony** – where one or more characters on stage are unaware of an important fact which we, the audience, know about, and which is somehow hinted at. For example, in Act 2, scene 3, the Porter jokes about being Porter of Hell. He doesn't know what we know: that Duncan is lying freshly murdered. Sometimes one character does know. For example, when Macbeth plans to murder Banquo and says to him, *Fail not our feast,* Banquo replies, *My lord, I will not.* There is a double irony here. We know, and Macbeth knows, Macbeth's plans. If we have read or seen the play, we also know what Macbeth cannot know – namely, that Banquo will indeed be at the feast, but as a ghost.

2 **Simple irony** – the sort used by Lennox here to express a meaning other than the apparent one. (He pretends to believe in Macbeth's innocence.)

Test yourself

? When and why does Macbeth feel *cabin'd, cribb'd, confin'd, bound in/ To saucy doubts and fears* (scene 4)?

? Imagine you are a guest at the banquet. Describe to a friend what took place and what it made you think. If working with a partner, role-play two guests in discussion.

? Write down something ironic that Lennox says about Macbeth in scene 6. Then write down something that he might say if he were just being sarcastic. What's the difference between the two lines?

time for the interval and refreshments!

Act 4 *scene* 1

◆ Witches cast ingredients of magic potion into cauldron.
◆ They show Macbeth three apparitions.
◆ Lennox brings news that Macduff has fled to England.
◆ Macbeth decides to kill Macduff's wife and children.

'**F**ire burn and cauldron bubble'

The Witches prepare a spell to summon spirits for Macbeth. The foul ingredients they throw into their boiling cauldron suggest poisonous evil, savagery, darkness, death and destruction. Which ones stand out in your mind?

In a speech probably not written by Shakespeare, Hecate congratulates the Witches on their efforts (*pains*).

The apparitions

The 2nd Witch feels in her thumbs that Macbeth is coming. He enters and ask what they're doing. ✪ What does the answer, *A deed without a name*, suggest to you?

Macbeth is shown three apparitions. What do you think each one means?
Read the suggested explanations on p. 56, then turn back to the picture and
test yourself.

Macbeth's speech beginning *I conjure you, by that which you profess* (line 50) seems halfway between an appeal and a command. He does not care anymore what destruction the Witches bring about, so long as they answer his questions. His words paint a picture of destruction by winds and waves that is so wild that even destruction itself (personified), grows sick.

The Witches agree to answer Macbeth's questions. They show him three apparitions of spirits:

1 **An armed head**. It could suggest military threat, or the head of Macbeth, cut off at the end of the play. It warns Macbeth to beware Macduff.
2 **A bloody child**. Macbeth, perhaps encouraged by the first spirit, attempts a joke: *Had I three ears, I'd hear thee*. The spirit tells him he has nothing to fear from any man *of woman born*. This reassures him. What he does not know (until the final scene of the play) is that Macduff was born by Caesarean (cut from his mother's womb), so in a sense he was not *of woman born*. The child could be Macduff – or his son.
3 **A crowned child with a tree**. This suggests Malcolm, soon to be king, who in Act 5, scene 5 orders his soldiers to cut down trees and carry them as a disguise. This spirit tells Macbeth he cannot be defeated until Birnam wood comes to Dunsinane. Macbeth thinks this will never happen – but, of course, it does.

Macbeth now wants to know whether Banquo's descendants will rule Scotland. The Witches try to stop him asking, but now he is confident enough to threaten them with a curse. They show him a vision of eight kings, followed by Banquo's ghost. The last king holds a mirror, or crystal ball, showing even more kings.

 Macbeth is appalled: *What! will the line stretch out to the crack of doom?* (the dawning of Doomsday).

The Witches pretend to be puzzled by Macbeth's surprise and horror. ❂ Do you think they are sincere when they perform an *antick*, a comic dance, supposedly to cheer him up?

News of Macduff

Lennox enters and Macbeth asks if he has seen the Witches. Lennox hasn't.

Macbeth is becoming ever more *bloody, bold and resolute,* as he was advised by the second apparition. He thinks his mistake in the past has been to think too much before acting. He resolves to change: *... from this moment/ The very firstlings of my heart shall be/ The firstlings of my hand.* In other words, he will act as soon as he thinks. And the first thing he thinks of doing is to seize the castle of Macduff and kill anyone onnected with him.

STYLE AND LANGUAGE

Read the Witches' chant, beginning *Round about the cauldron go* (lines 4–38). It is in rhyming couplets and is in a different rhythm to most of the play.

There is a repeated refrain in which they all join in. Notice its rhyming and the power built up by the use of **alliteration** (the repetition of a sound at the beginning of words) – the repeated 'd' and 'b' sounds. ❍ What is the overall effect?

Act 4 *scene* 2

◆ Ross and Lady Macduff discuss Macduff's flight and Scotland's problems.
◆ Lady Macduff discusses her husband with her son.
◆ Messenger warns her she's in danger.
◆ Murderers arrive and kill Lady Macduff and her son.

Ross and Lady Macduff

This scene takes place in Macduff's castle in Fife. Lady Macduff complains that her husband must be mad, or without concern for his family, to have left them defenceless and fly to England. Even the wren, she says (a tiny bird), will fight an owl (significantly, a night bird) to protect her young.

Ross says he is leaving because otherwise he will disgrace himself by weeping. ❍ Why else might he want to leave?

'Was my father a traitor, mother?'

This part of the scene is full of horror and pathos. We see the simple and affectionate conversation between Macduff's son and his mother. We know from the previous scene what they don't know – that they are about to die.

The dramatic irony is increased by Lady Macduff's line, *Sirrah, your father's dead*. We know that although Macduff is not really dead, mother and son soon will be.

❂ Why does Lady Macduff say that her husband is dead? Is she testing her son? Does he take her seriously?

There is a sad humour in the conversation, especially when the boy says that *the liars and swearers are fools* to let themselves be hanged by the honest men, since the honest men are outnumbered.

The message and murder

A messenger arrives to warn Lady Macduff that she is in danger. After he's gone, she questions why she should run away when she's done nothing wrong. At the same time, she is aware that the world doesn't necessarily reward virtue.

Earlier in the scene, Lady Macduff has appeared to blame her husband for leaving his family unprotected. But when the murderers arrive, she returns at once to the role of loyal wife. When they ask where Macduff is she says she hopes he is *in no place so unsanctified* (unholy) that men like them could find him. She means they belong in hell.

Macduff's son bravely defends his father's name and with his last breath urges his mother to flee. ❂ Is this realistic?

It may seem strange that Shakespeare created the character of Lady Macduff only to kill her off after one scene. But think what a good contrast she is to Lady Macbeth. The scene also engages our sympathies, preventing us from becoming hardened to the awful events taking place.

Act 4 *scene* 3

◆ Malcolm expresses doubts about Macduff's loyalty.
◆ Malcolm tests Macduff by accusing himself.
◆ We hear of King Edward's healing powers.
◆ Ross brings news of Scotland, including murder of Macduff's family.

*M*alcolm doubts Macduff

This is the only scene set outside Scotland – at King Edward's palace. We see a contrast between Malcolm and Macduff. Malcolm suggests they find a good place to *Weep our sad bosoms empty.* Macduff says that instead they should fight to defend their country.

Malcolm distrusts Macduff at first. He points out that Macduff was once loyal to Macbeth, and that Macduff has not as yet suffered at Macbeth's hands. Therefore, it might make good sense for Macduff to seek Macbeth's approval by betraying Malcolm.

Macduff's simple, straightforward answer is in character: *I am not treacherous.* Malcolm says he's sorry to have to doubt Macduff. After all, just because some people seem trustworthy and turn out not to be, it doesn't mean that no one who appears trustworthy actually is.

Malcolm's special reason for doubting Macduff is that Macduff apparently thought it safe to leave his family unprotected. There is **dramatic irony** here (see p. 53). ❂ What do we know that they don't? If Macduff left his family unprotected, this might mean that he was Macbeth's ally and therefore had nothing to fear from him.

Malcolm accuses himself

Malcolm apparently decides to test Macduff's loyalty. He does it by accusing himself of so many sins – lust, greed, and destructiveness – that he seems totally unfit to be a king. In fact, Macduff eventually says that Malcolm isn't even fit to live.

This is the answer that Malcolm had hoped for. ✪ What might Macduff have said instead, if he'd been dishonest or treacherous?

Malcolm reassures Macduff that in fact he's a virgin, has never told a lie, and is not greedy or treacherous. What does Malcolm's trick make you feel about him? Will he make a good king?

The healer king

The next bit of the scene is sometimes cut in productions of the play, because it is not essential to the action. We hear of how King Edward has a strange power to cure people of *the Evil*, a form of tuberculosis, and how he has *a heavenly gift of prophecy*. Although not vital to the story, it forms a good contrast to Macbeth. ✪ Does Macbeth cure anyone? What sort of prophecy is he associated with?

✪ Do you think Shakespeare really believed in the special powers of a true king, or was he just flattering King James I?

News from Scotland

Ross appears once again as messenger. He says things have got so bad in Scotland that *the dead man's knell/ Is there scarce ask'd for who*. (So many are dying that when the bell is rung for a death, people hardly bother asking anymore who it's for.)

Ross cannot bring himself at first to tell Macduff about the massacre of his family. When he does, Macduff cannot take in the awful news. He is in a state of shock, as his repeated questions show:

> *My children too?*
> *My wife kill'd too?*
> *All my pretty ones?*
> *Did you say all? ... All?*
> *What, all my pretty chickens and their dam*
> *At one fell swoop?*

Notice that he calls Macbeth a *hell-kite,* a bird of prey that would swoop down and kill the *pretty chickens* (Macduff's children).

Malcolm encourages Macduff to *let grief/ Convert to anger,* and this is what Macduff in fact does. He vows to kill Macbeth.

Test yourself

? What three apparitions do the Witches show Macbeth (*scene 1*)? Draw something to suggest each one in the boxes below. Write a note on what each means beneath your drawing.

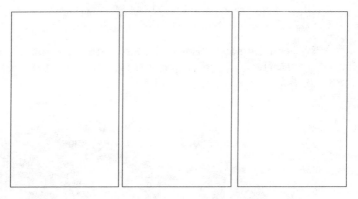

? Ross says Macduff is *noble, wise, judicious* (scene 2). Do you agree? What justifications can you think of for Macduff's flight?

? In what ways are Lady Macbeth and Lady Macduff different? Show the differences in a Mind Map. Use adjectives to describe each woman. What words can be applied to both?

? Of what sins does Malcolm accuse himself (scene 3)? Try to think of mental images for them.

now take a break before looking in on Lady Macbeth

Act 5 *scene* 1

◆ Doctor and lady-in-waiting discuss Lady Macbeth.
◆ Lady Macbeth walks and talks in sleep. Tries to wash hands.
◆ Doctor says he can't cure her.

This scene takes place in Dunsinane Castle. It shows a much-changed Lady Macbeth. Previously a powerful, commanding woman, now she is broken and pitiable. Her sleep-talking and repetitive hand-washing show that she is suffering unbearably from her sense of guilt. These things also make it clear to the doctor and gentlewoman that Lady Macbeth has been involved in murder.

The gentlewoman reports that she has seen Lady Macbeth write a letter. ❂ What do you think she's written? A confession? A letter to her husband? A letter warning Lady Macduff?

The gentlewoman refuses to tell the doctor what she has heard Lady Macbeth say, so long as there is no witness to back her up. ❂ Why do you think this is?

Do you now feel any sympathy for Lady Macbeth?

Lady Macbeth carries a candle. We hear that *she has light by her continually*. She has become afraid of the dark, like a child. She seems to wash her hands in her sleep. We know for certain what the gentlewoman and doctor can only suspect: that she is trying to wash away her guilt, symbolised by the imagined blood on her hands. When she says, *all the perfumes of Arabia will not sweeten this little hand*, she seems a pathetic figure.

 The beginning of the doctor's final speech echoes the earlier reports of unnatural events: *Unnatural deeds/ Do breed unnatural troubles*. He blames Lady Macbeth's illness on this.

STYLE AND LANGUAGE

Read Lady Macbeth's speeches. They are broken, disjointed, suggesting sleep-walking and madness. They are the words of a broken woman. The little rhyme, *The Thane of Fife had a wife*, is childlike, as if she is retreating into second childhood.

She speaks in prose. Verse would seem inappropriate for the disjointed ramblings of a sick mind. Perhaps it is simply in keeping with the mood of the scene that the gentlewoman and doctor speak in prose, although the doctor's one long speech is in verse. ❂ What do you think is passing through her mind?

Act 5 *scene 2*

◆ Scottish lords discuss the enemy, Macbeth, as they lead their soldiers to join Malcolm's forces.

The scene takes place near Macbeth's castle. From this point, the action of the play speeds up. Short scenes cut between the opposing armies.

We hear that some people now call Macbeth mad, while others still think he shows *valiant fury*. Some of his followers are revolting against him, while those who stay with him do so only out of fear, not loyalty.

STYLE AND LANGUAGE

Clothing images often appear in the play. Now Angus says of Macbeth:

... now does he feel his title
Hang loose about him, like a giant's robe
Upon a dwarfish thief.

Try to picture this in your mind. Macbeth may be king in name, but in reality he is not big enough to wear that title.

Act 5 *scene* 3

◆ Servant tells Macbeth that English army has come.
◆ Macbeth questions doctor about Lady Macbeth while putting on armour.

Macbeth is in his castle preparing for battle. His mood swings wildly. At first, he seems defiantly confident, reassuring himself with the Witches' prophecies. His castle is safe *Till Birnam wood remove to Dunsinane* and he cannot be killed by *man that's born of woman*. Then a servant tells him that the English army is at hand, and he is thrown into a fury, cursing and taunting the unfortunate youth for looking pale with fear. He tells him to prick his face and spread blood on his cheeks for colour.

In lines 11–17 Macbeth throws four insults at the servant about his pale face. ● What are they?

Macbeth seems manic. He interrupts himself: *I am sick at heart/ When I behold – Seyton, I say!* Yet he is determined to fight to the death if necessary: *I'll fight till from my bones my flesh be hack'd*. He insists on putting on his armour, even though it is not needed yet (line 34).

Macbeth, though desperate, is in command. He fires orders, and at one point he gives four in a row: *Send out more horses, skirr the country round;/ Hang those that talk of fear. Give me mine armour* (lines 35–6). Notice how he moves rapidly in the last sentence from dealing with the situation to getting his armour on. He then shifts in the same breath to questioning the doctor about Lady Macbeth: *How does your patient, doctor?*

He loses patience with medicine: *Throw physic to the dogs; I'll none of it.* Yet he seems to ask the doctor's advice about Scotland's sickness (lines 50–6), interrupting himself again to tell Seyton to pull off his armour again. He hardly listens to the reply. In fact, he seems to ignore it. His *Bring it after me* refers to the armour just pulled off.

The doctor's final aside is Shakespeare's little joke at the expense of doctors, who were thought of as money-grabbing.

Now try this

? Write a short speech in the style of sleep-walking Lady Macbeth. Speak it aloud.

? Imagine you are directing the play. Write brief notes on Macbeth's main mood swings in scene 3 and how they should be acted.

Act 5 *scene* 4

◆ Macbeth's enemies approach.
◆ Malcolm orders his soldiers each to cut a branch and carry it.

This is another short, active scene. Malcolm approaches with the combined English and Scottish army. He orders his soldiers to cut down branches from Birnam wood and carry them to conceal their numbers from Macbeth.

❂ What prophecy does this fulfil?

Malcolm says that those who fight on Macbeth's side do so only because they have been forced to. Their *hearts are absent.*

Siward warns Malcolm against over-optimism, saying that only the coming battle itself can decide the outcome. This contrasts with Macbeth's desperate clinging to the Witches' prophecies.

Act 5 *scene* 5

◆ Macbeth boasts that his castle will withstand a siege.
◆ Seyton brings Macbeth news of Lady Macbeth's death.
◆ A messenger tells Macbeth that Birnam wood is approaching.

This scene takes us back inside Macbeth's castle. At first he is still hopeful, insisting that his castle is strong enough to *laugh a siege to scorn* so that the attackers will die of hunger and sickness before they manage to break in.

From off-stage there comes a noise, which Seyton tells Macbeth is *the cry of women*. In Macbeth's reaction, we see now how much he has changed since earlier on in the play when he was so fearful of being found out, and so terrified by Banquo's ghost. He comments that he has *almost forgot the taste of fears* because he has *supp'd full with horrors*. In other words, he is so used to horror that he is no longer fearful.

'The queen, my lord, is dead'

When Macbeth hears that the women's cry was in response to Lady Macbeth's death, he sinks into a mood of bitter despair. The speech beginning *She should have died hereafter* (lines 17–28) is an important one, worth your reading again now.

'Tomorrow, and tomorrow, and tomorrow'

❂ What do you think Macbeth means in this line? Some critics think he is saying that Lady Macbeth would have died eventually anyway – as if he doesn't really care. Others think he is wishing that her death could have been delayed – perhaps until after the battle. How much do you think he really cares abut her?

In the rest of the speech Macbeth sees the days ahead creeping on pointlessly to *the last syllable of recorded time*, as if to the end of a book. All the previous days in history (*all our yesterdays*) have provided only enough light for fools (all mankind) to see their way to death, like a candle lighting our way to bed. He sees life as being like a candle that burns only for a short time. (Think of the mad Lady Macbeth insisting on having a candle burning by her through the night.)

In a second image he compares life to an actor's brief appearance on stage. Finally, he sees life as a *tale/ Told by an idiot*. It seems important, but in fact it is meaningless.

❂ Think about the three images of life. How effective do you find each one?

Birnam wood

The mood of grim despair is broken by the news that Birnam wood is approaching Dunsinane. ❂ Can you remember how? (If not, look back to the previous scene.) Macbeth's reaction is a mixture of disbelief and desperate anger. He threatens the messenger, but then begins to suspect that the devil (*the fiend*), through the Witches, has tricked him with *equivocation .../ That lies like truth* – with ambiguous words that conceal the truth.

There is despair in the line *I 'gin to be aweary of the sun.* None the less, Macbeth is determined to go down fighting: *Blow, wind! come, wrack!/ At least we'll die with harness on our back.* (Harness is armour.) Notice the **rhyming couplet** (a pair of rhyming lines, often used at the end of a speech), giving a sense of determination. See if you can find others at the ends of speeches between here and the end of the play.

Act 5 *scene* 6

◆ Malcolm's army prepares for battle.

In this, the shortest scene of the play, Malcolm orders his soldiers to throw down their branches, cut in Birnam wood. Siward is to lead the attack; Malcolm and Macduff will follow.

Macduff orders the trumpets to be sounded.

Act 5 *scene* 7

◆ Battle rages. Macbeth kills Young Siward.
◆ Macduff tells Macbeth he was not *of woman born.* They fight.
◆ Ross tells Siward that his son (Young Siward) is dead.
◆ Macduff enters with Macbeth's head.
◆ Malcolm announces that he will be crowned at Scone.

In some versions of the play, this scene is broken into three separate scenes. These are shown by the headings that follow.

Young Siward dies

Macbeth has left his castle to fight in the open. Using another animal image, he compares himself to a bear tied to a stake: he has no choice but to fight.

Young Siward appears and challenges Macbeth. They fight and Young Siward dies. With a trace of very grim humour, Macbeth tells the lifeless youth, *Thou wast born of woman*. How does he know?

Macbeth exits, and Macduff enters looking for him. Macduff cannot bring himself to attack *wretched* mercenaries. He has no quarrel with them, only with Macbeth.

Macduff exits, and Malcolm and Old Siward enter. Siward says that the castle has been surrendered, and that Malcolm's army has almost won (*The day almost itself professes yours*). Malcolm comments that some of Macbeth's army are now fighting against Macbeth.

'Turn, hell-hound, turn!'

Alone on stage for a moment, Macbeth says that he won't commit suicide, as a Roman might have done to avoid dishonourable capture, but will fight on.

Macduff enters, sees Macbeth, and challenges him: *Turn, hell-hound, turn!* At first, Macbeth refuses to fight, on the grounds that he has already spilt too much of Macduff's blood (his family). Macduff can't accept this, and they fight. When Macbeth says that Macduff is wasting his time because he can't be killed by *one of woman born*, Macduff tells Macbeth to despair, because he, Macduff, was born by Caesarean.

Macbeth momentarily loses his spirit. He says that Macduff has taken his courage away (*... cow'd my better part of man*). He now no longer believes *these juggling fiends* who have given him false hope. He does not want to fight, but Macduff threatens him with being put on show like a caged animal.

Macbeth's final speech is proudly defiant. He declares, *Yet I will try my last*. In other words, he will fight to the death.

Remember the first Thane of Cawdor, whose execution is reported by Malcolm in Act 1, scene 4: *Nothing in his life/ Became him like the leaving it.* ✪ Does this now seem true of Macbeth? How do you feel about Macbeth as he makes his last exit? Is he in any sense a hero?

Malcolm's victory

Ross breaks the news of Young Siward's death. Old Siward takes it in a soldierly way, asking only if his son had his wounds on the front of his body – indicating that he died facing the enemy.

Who's the hero?

Macduff enters with Macbeth's head, and hails Malcolm as King. He says that now *the time is free*. This could mean that the age in which they live is now free, or that time itself has been standing still while Scotland has been gripped in a nightmare.

Notice that in victory Malcolm behaves rather like his father Duncan in Act 1, scene 4. Like Duncan, he bestows honours (*Henceforth be earls*) and thanks all those who have helped to win victory. He even uses the image of planting once used by Duncan: *Which would be planted newly with the time.* Whereas Macbeth was associated with blood and death, Malcolm, like his father Duncan, is associated with his country's healthy growth.

STYLE AND LANGUAGE

Blank verse, used for most speeches in the play, is iambic pentameter, which means most lines have five pairs of syllables. Sometimes a line is shared between two speeches, showing some connection between two characters. This happens in line 42:

Macbeth: *To one of woman born.*
Macduff: *Despair thy thy charm.*

Tap out and count the syllables to check this. Compare this with line 45: *Untimely ripp'd.* On hearing this, we might for a moment expect the line to be continued, but it isn't. ✪ How does this short line, surprising us by its sudden end, fit its sense?

Test yourself

? Below is the *Fife Times* countdown of events leading up to Malcolm's victory, which a junior editor has got in the wrong order. Can you put it right? (To see how you've done, check summaries for scenes 4–7.)

- Macduff challenges Macbeth.
- Macbeth claims his castle will stand a siege.
- Macduff enters with Macbeth's head.
- Macbeth told Birnam wood on the move.
- Malcolm orders men to cut and carry branches.
- Malcolm's army prepares for battle.
- Old Siward hears of son's death.
- Macbeth's enemies approach Dunsinane.
- Malcolm announces forthcoming coronation.

- Young Siward killed.
- Lady Macbeth commits suicide.
- Battle begins.

? Can you spot the factual inaccuracies in the *Fife Times* report below?

DEATH OF A TYRANT

There was rejoicing last night at the news that the tyrant Macbeth was dead. He died in a man-to-man fight outside his castle at Forres with our glorious new king, Malcolm.

Macbeth, who inherited the title Thane of Cawdor from his father, persuaded the late King Duncan's servants to kill their master. Later, he poisoned his former friend Banquo and his son Fleance at a banquet. He also ordered the murder of Macduff's family. Eventually, trusting no one, he even hanged his own wife.

At the time of his death, the cowardly Macbeth was trying to escape to Norway. Luckily for Scotland, he never made it.

CORRECTIONS TO 'DEATH OF A TYRANT'

- Macbeth was killed by Macduff at Dunsinane.
- He was made Thane of Cawdor by Duncan.
- He killed Duncan himself.
- He arranged for Banquo and Fleance to be murdered while they were out riding, but Fleance escaped.
- Lady Macbeth killed herself.
- Macbeth did not try to escape.

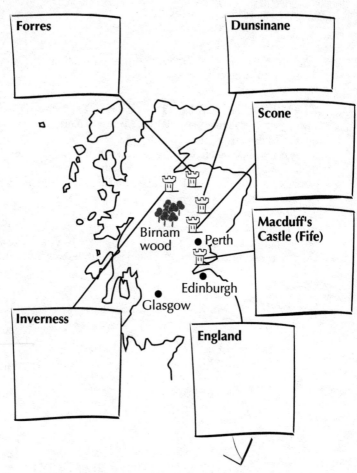

Forres

Dunsinane

Scone

Macduff's Castle (Fife)

Birnam wood

Perth

Edinburgh

Glasgow

Inverness

England

? Fill in the boxes with the key events that occur in each place. Check the stage directions at the beginning of each scene to see how you've done. Only one place does not appear in a stage direction. Which one? Why?

if you've worked carefully through the whole Commentary, you should be well on the way to an 'A'. For now, take a break!

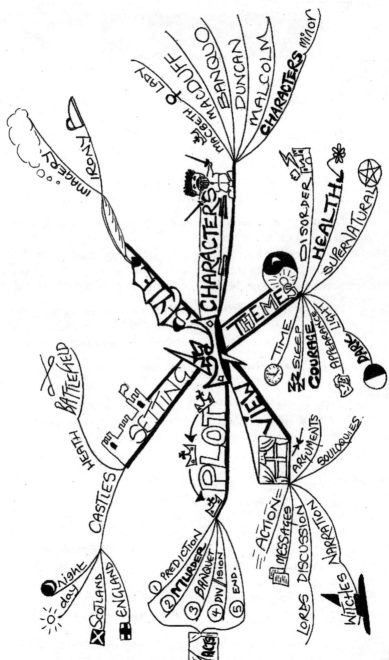

73

TOPICS FOR DISCUSSION AND BRAINSTORMING

One of the best ways to revise is with one or more friends. Even if you're with someone who hardly knows the text you're studying, you'll find that having to explain things to your friend will help you to organise your own thoughts and memorise key points. If you're with someone who has studied the text, you'll find that the things you can't remember are different to the things your friend can't remember – so you'll help each other.

Discussion will also help you to develop interesting new ideas that perhaps neither of you would have had alone. Use a **brainstorming** approach to tackle any of the topics listed below. Allow yourself to share whatever ideas come into your head – however silly they seem. This will get you thinking creatively.

Whether alone or with a friend, use Mind Mapping (see p. vi) to help you brainstorm and organise your ideas. If with a friend, use a large sheet of paper and thick coloured pens.

Here are some typical questions that could feature in your exam or be set for coursework.

1 Is Macbeth basically a good man led astray?
2 How does Macbeth change as the play progresses?
3 Is Lady Macbeth a loyal and supportive wife?
4 Is Macduff perfect?
5 What roles do Macduff and Malcolm play in Macbeth's overthrow?
6 Will Malcolm make a good king?
7 In *Macbeth* the villains are much more exciting than the good characters. Is this true?
8 Discuss the role of the supernatural in the play.
9 What lessons can we learn about power from the play?
10 Write epitaphs for all the characters who die in the play.
11 How important is humour in *Macbeth*?
12 How does Shakespeare use animal imagery in the play?

In all your study, in coursework, and in exams, be aware of the following:

- **Characterisation** – the characters and how we know about them (e.g. what they say and do, how the author describes them), their relationships, and how they develop.
- **Plot and structure** – what happens and how it is organised into parts or episodes.
- **Setting and atmosphere** – the changing scene and how it reflects the story (e.g. a rugged landscape and storm reflecting a character's emotional difficulties).
- **Style and language** – the author's choice of words, and literary devices such as imagery, and how these reflect the mood.
- **Viewpoint** – how the story is told (e.g. through an imaginary narrator, or in the third person but through the eyes of one character – 'She was furious – how dare he!').
- **Social and historical context** – influences on the author (see 'Background' in this guide).

Develop your ability to:

- Relate **detail** to **broader content, meaning and style**.
- Show understanding of the author's **intentions, technique and meaning** (brief and appropriate comparisons with other works by the same author will gain marks).
- Give **personal response and interpretation**, backed up by **examples** and short **quotations**.
- **Evaluate** the author's achievement (how far does the author succeed and why?)

The last chapter gives an example of an A-grade exam essay, with the Mind Map and sequence used to plan it. Take careful note of the numbered points: they tell you what's good about the essay.

THE EXAM ESSAY

Planning

You will probably have about an hour for one essay. It is worth spending about ten minutes planning it. An excellent way to do this is in the three stages below.

1 **Mind Map** your ideas, without worrying about their order yet.
2 **Order** the relevant ideas (the ones that really relate to the question) by numbering them in the order in which you will write the essay.
3 **Gather** your evidence and short quotes.

You could remember this as the **MOG** technique.

Writing and checking

Then write the essay, allowing five minutes at the end for checking relevance, and spelling, grammar and punctuation.

Remember!

Stick to the question, and always **back up** your points with evidence in the form of examples and short quotations. Note: you can use '. . .' for unimportant words missed out in a quotation.

Model answer and plans

The next (and final) chapter consists of a model answer to an exam question on *Macbeth*, followed by Mind Maps and essay plans. Don't be put off if you think you couldn't write an essay as good as this one yet. This is a top 'A' grade essay – a standard at which to aim. You'll develop your skills if you work at them. Even if you're reading this the night before the exam, you can easily memorise the MOG technique in order to do your personal best.

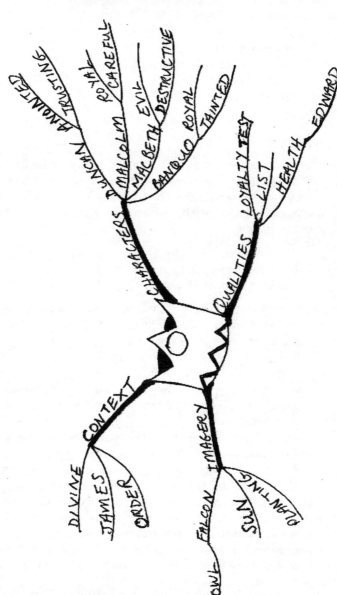

How is kingship presented in Macbeth?

PLAN

1 Context: Divine Right, social order, regicide.
2 Qualities of Kingship:
   (a) Malcolm's list and test;
   (b) Edward the healer King.
3 Characters – how kingly is each?
   (a) Duncan and Malcolm;
   (b) Macbeth and Banquo.
4 Imagery.

ESSAY

In Shakespeare's time, most people believed in the Divine
Right of kings: kings were thought to be appointed by God to
preserve the social order. Thus, Duncan's murder is a crime
against God and society,[1] which is why Macduff says, on
discovering it:

> 'Confusion now hath made his masterpiece!
> Most sacrilegious murder hath broke ope
> The Lord's anointed temple.[2]'

Here confusion (chaos) and murder are personified. Confusion
destroys the order created by God. The temple is the body of
Duncan, anointed at his coronation.[3]

In Act 4, scene 3, when Malcolm tests Macduff's loyalty by
pretending to be unfit to be king, he lists what he sees as the
'king-becoming graces'. These are justice, truthfulness,
moderation, stability, generosity, perseverance, mercy, humility,
devotion, patience, courage, and strength of character.[4] This
gives us a yardstick against which to measure the play's three
kings – Duncan, Malcolm and Macbeth.

A fourth king, the English Edward, does not actually appear
in the play, but his powers of healing and prophecy are
described. Shakespeare probably included this description
partly to flatter James I, who thought he had inherited these
powers spiritually from Edward.[5] It is not essential to the play,
and allows the pace of the scene to sag.[6] However, it does
form a contrast to Macbeth, who brings sickness to his country,

and to the evil, 'equivocating' prophecies of the Witches.

Duncan certainly has kingly 'graces'.[7] He appreciates those who fight on his side, and he has the humility to thank them. He also shows justice in punishing treachery and rewarding noble deeds.

Even Macbeth admits that Duncan has been an excellent king, 'clear in his great office'.[8]

If Duncan has faults, they are that he is too trusting, and does not distribute rewards fairly. He is taken in by the treacherous Thane of Cawdor and by Macbeth, and he rewards only Macbeth, not the equally deserving Banquo.

Malcolm shows similar virtues to his father. The link between them is also made clear by imagery. Both talk about 'planting' good men and good deeds, so that they may grow healthily.[9] However, Malcolm is less trusting, as is shown by his testing of Macduff's loyalty, and in his final speech he makes his 'thanes and kinsmen' earls, rather than just honouring one man.

Macbeth does not seem to have the first two vices that Malcolm accuses himself of – lustfulness and greed, but he is solely concerned with his own power, not his country's well-being. He becomes a hated tyrant, who keeps spies in every household and rules by fear. His cruelty is shown by his massacre of Macduff's family.[10]

Macbeth is essentially a soldier, not a king. He fears Banquo's 'royalty of nature' not only because Banquo might expose him, and because the Witches have predicted that Banquo's descendants will be kings (James I was one of them), but because he knows that Banquo would make a better king than him.[11] In murdering Duncan, he is like the owl that the Old Man says has killed a falcon (a royal bird), or like night strangling the sun, another symbol of kingship (Act 2, scene 4).[12]

In Act 5, scene 2, Angus compares Macbeth to a 'dwarfish thief' who feels his kingship 'Hang loose about him, like a giant's robe'.[13] He is unworthy of his stolen throne. When he is replaced by Malcolm, a worthy king, the social order is restored.[14]

WHAT'S SO GOOD ABOUT IT?

1 Relevant use of historical context.
2 Good use of quote to back up point.
3 Understanding of text.
4 Gives a sound basis for assessment and shows understanding.
5 Relevant background knowledge.
6 Ability to evaluate.
7 Refers back to an earlier point.
8 Good use of quote.
9 Understanding of kingship, and imagery.
10 Good use of an example.
11 Interesting interpretation.
12 Grasp of relevant imagery.
13 Good, selective use of quoted image.
14 Good conclusion, drawing ideas together without waffle.

And on the next pages you will find one more essay plan, with the Mind Map used to brainstorm it.

Is *Lady Macbeth the real villain in* Macbeth?

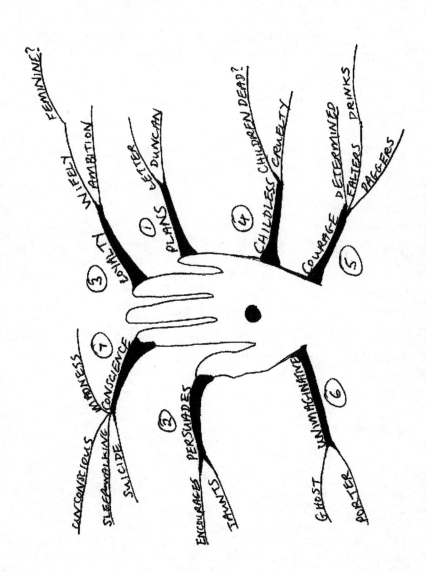

PLAN

1 Assumes Duncan's murder necessary; plans.
2 Persuades Macbeth.
3 Loyal wife – ambitious only for husband? Denies femininity ('unsex me here').
4 Childless: children dead? Bitter? 'I have given suck' speech.
5 Courage, determination. Dutch courage. Retrieves bloody daggers.
6 Unimaginative?
7 Guilty conscience leads to madness and suicide. Pitiable in the end.

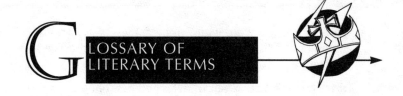

GLOSSARY OF LITERARY TERMS

alliteration   repetition of a sound at the beginnings of words, e.g. *burn, bubble.*

aside   a short speech spoken by one character, as if thinking aloud, not meant to be heard by others on stage.

blank verse   the kind of non-rhyming verse, with five pairs of syllables to each line, in which Shakespeare usually writes. Also called **iambic pentameter**.

context   the social and historical influences on the author.

couplet   *see* **rhyming couplet**.

dramatic irony   *see* **irony (dramatic)**

hero   *see* **tragic hero**.

image   a word picture used to make an idea come alive; e.g. a **metaphor**, **simile**, or **personification** (see separate entries).

imagery   the kind of word picture used to make an idea come alive.

irony   **(dramatic)** where at least one character on stage is unaware of an important fact which the audience knows about, and which is somehow hinted at; **(simple)** ridiculing an opinion or belief by pretending to hold it, or pretending to be ignorant of the true facts.

metaphor   a description of a thing as if it were something essentially different but also in some way similar; e.g. Duncan's servants *badg'd with blood* – the bloodstains are like badges (see also p. 34).

personification   a description of something abstract as if it were a person; e.g *Confusion now hath made his masterpiece!* (see also p. 34).

prose   language in which, unlike verse, there is no set number of syllables in a line, and no rhyming.

pun   a use of a word with two meanings, or of two similar-sounding words, where both meanings are appropriate in different ways.

rhyming couplet   a pair of rhyming lines, often used at the end of a speech.

simile   a comparison of two things which are different in most ways but similar in one important way; e.g. *signs of nobleness, like stars* (see also p. 34)

theme   an idea explored by an author; e.g. time

tragedy   a play focusing on a tragic hero (see separate entry)

tragic hero   a character whose nobility or achievement we admire, and whose downfall and death through a weakness or error, coupled with fate, arouses our sympathy.

setting   the place in which the action occurs, which usually affects the atmosphere; e.g. the moor where the Witches meet.

structure   how the plot is organised.

viewpoint   how the story is told; e.g. through action, or in discussion between minor characters.

INDEX

Page references in bold denote major
character or theme sections

Angus   18, 35
appearances   **25–6**, 36, 37–8, 56, 60, 65
Banquo   **15–16**
   courage 15, 32
   ghost of 23, 24, 26, 50–2, 56
   murder 28, 48, 50
   son Fleance 40, 50
   suspicions 16, 34, 35, 40, 46, 47
   virtues 15–16, 34, 47
Birnam wood 56, 64, 65, 67, 72
Cawdor, Thane of (old) 36
courage   **26–7**, 36, 59, 69 (*see also under*
   Banquo; Macbeth; Macbeth,
   Lady; Macduff)
disorder   **21–2**
   imagery 22
   and loyalty 21, 58, 59
   nature 21, 22, 44, 63
   social 21–2, 49, 52
Doctors 22, 23, 62–3, 65
Donalbain 19
Duncan   **18**
   murdered 41–4
   character 18, 22, 36, 38, 40, 70, 79
Edward, King 1, 23, 24, 60, 78
   imagery
   animal 27, 49, 68
   blood and water 24, 33, 45
   clothing 26, 34–5, 39, 64
   devices 33–4
   disorder 22
James I, King 1, 60, 78, 79
kingship 1, 21, 78–9
Lennox 18, 22, 44, 53, 56
light and dark (theme)   **24–5**, 46–7, 49, 50,
   52, 63, 66
Macbeth (the character)   **8–12**
   ambition 11, 36
   conscience 9, 28, 42, 47
   courage 8–9, 26, 27, 32–4, 52, 63, 68–9
   death 69
   development 11, 49
   dishonesty 25, 40, 45
   fears 9, 10, 51–2, 66
   moods 64–5, 66–7
   murders 9, 10, 21–2, 35, 38–9, 41, 42,
    46–8, 57, 79
   unworthiness 26, 35, 64, 79
Macbeth, Lady   **13–15**
   ambition 13, 37, 39

childlessness 14
courage 27, 41, 66
dishonesty 25, 38, 45
fears 13, 41, 48
imagination 14, 42, 43
madness 14, 15, 24, 25, 42, 62–3
spirits, summons 13, 23
suicide 27, 66
taunts Macbeth 14, 26, 39, 52
will-power 13, 15
Macdonwald 21
Macduff   **16–17**
   action 16, 44, 67, 68
   Caesarean birth 68
   courage 27, 68
   grief 61
   humour 16, 44
   loyalty 17, 22, 59–60, 78
Macduff, Lady 18, 27, (and son) 57–9
Malcolm   **18**
   Cumberland, Duke of 36
   flight 18
   health, and 22, 78
   loyalty test 18, 25, 60, 78
   order, and 18, 22, 29, 69
   suspicion 18, 25, 59, 79
   tactics 25, 65, 67
Porter 43–4
Ross 18, 22, 28, 32, 35, 57, 60
Sergeant 32, 33–4
settings 31–2, 38, 72
Seyton 64, 66
sickness and health   **22–3**, 36, 38, 60, 63, 65
sleep   **27–8**, 34, 40, 41, 42, 49, 52
style and language
   alliteration 37, 57
imagery 24, 26, 27, 33–5, 39, 41, 45,
   49, 64, 68
   irony 43, 53–4
   prose 43
   puns 34–5
   verse 32, 37, 39, 43–4, 52–3, 57, 70
supernatural, the 1, 13, **23–4**, 65, 67
   (*see also* Banquo, ghost of; Witches)
time   **28–9**, 38, 40, 44, 56, 66, 69
tragic hero defined 8
witchcraft, belief in 1
Witches
   evil nature 19, 23, 25
   and Hecate 23, 52–3
   prediction 23–4, 28, 34, 54–6, 64, 65
   spells 32, 34, 54–6, 57

BUZAN TRAINING COURSES

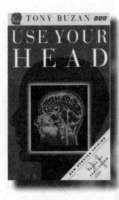

For further information on books, video and audio tapes,
support materials and courses, please send for
our brochure.

Buzan Centres Ltd, 54 Parkstone Road, Poole, Dorset, BH15 2PX
Tel: 44 (0) 1202 674676, Fax: 44 (0) 1202 674776
Email: Buzan_Centres_Ltd@compuserve.com